Contents

Acknowledgements   iv

Introduction   vi

1 Skin   1
2 Hair   35
3 Make-up   78
4 Diet is not a dirty word   109
5 Exercise is not a specialist field   124

Acknowledgements

The authors and publishers wish to acknowledge, with thanks,
the following photographic sources.
Alex by Ben of Brixton   pp 38; 39
BBC Hulton Picture Library   p 69
Karl Finn   p 37   Courtesy Jenny Cooper
Sally and Richard Greenhill   pp 12; 13
Newton Harris   pp 40   Courtesy Margaret Boateng;   41
Courtesy Curl Up and Dye Salon;   100
Chandana Juliet Highet   pp v; vii right; 16; 36 bottom; 44;
55; 68; 78; 79; 82; 108; cover photograph
James Hipkiss   pp 1; 34; 125; 126; 127
Alan Hutchison Library   p vii left, 36 top, photographs
Chandana Juliet Highet
Popperfoto   p vi
The publishers have made every effort to trace the copyright
holders, but if they have inadvertently overlooked any, they
will be pleased to make the necessary arrangements at the
first opportunity.

The Black Book of
Beauty

Barbara Jackson and Lydia Eagle

MACMILLAN

© Copyright text Barbara Jackson and Lydia Eagle, 1984
© Copyright illustrations The Macmillan Press Ltd, 1984

First published 1984
Reprinted 1986, 1988, 1992 (twice)

Published by THE MACMILLAN PRESS LTD
London and Basingstoke
Associated companies and representatives in Accra,
Auckland, Delhi, Dublin, Gaborone, Hamburg, Harare,
Hong Kong, Kuala Lumpur, Lagos, Manzini, Melbourne,
Mexico City, Nairobi, New York, Singapore, Tokyo.

ISBN 0-333-36865-7

Printed in Hong Kong

I have known the women of many lands and nations, I have known and seen and lived beside them, but none have I known more sweetly feminine, more unswervingly loyal, more desperately earnest, and more instinctively pure in body and in soul, than the daughters of my Black mothers.

W.E.B. DuBois

Introduction

Down through recorded history, and in legend, the 'exotic' beauty of the black woman has long been celebrated, for we are the daughters of Cleopatra and the sisters of Sheba. The uniqueness of women like Cleo Laine, Maya Angelou, Coretta King, Miriam Makeba, to name just a few, has been recognised. Some of these women have been famous, some unknown. Their beauty has not been superficial, but has combined strength and character. Now, for the first time in history, the black

Eartha Kitt

woman has come into her own. She lives in an age where narrow, restricted ideas of beauty have been replaced by a much more individual look. She can be the woman she wants to be — and *SHE* decides. Not only does she have more money to spend on herself, but she is better educated, works at a variety of jobs and professions, travels more, and willingly spends time and money on her appearance. She is now free to look like herself. The days of outrageous clothes and weird make-up are truly in the past.

A generation or so ago, whether one grew up in Africa, America, Europe or the Caribbean, there was no such thing as a 'black' model girl; well, not exactly, that is. There was nobody identifiably black that one could relate to as a 'sister'. Certainly from time to time a girl was taken up and treated as a novelty, for a while, and then disappeared. The concept of make-up for black women, or their participation in anything but the entertainment world, was unthought of, or at least unacceptable, despite

Edna Mosheshe

Miriam Makeba

the fact that black women trained for the professions, practised law, medicine and taught in schools. Her public image was always that of either earth mother or sex object – as opposed to sex symbol. This self-fulfilling myth was advanced and rigidly enforced by the population at large. We were thought of as 'exotic', whether we liked it or not. Eartha Kitt was actually the first black woman to be universally thought of as a sex symbol. The standard of beauty had always been: light skin, 'good' (straight) hair and nose to match. Women 'fried' their hair and tried to bleach their skins in an attempt to be 'beautiful'. If you had 'bad' (kinky) hair, and were black, you were in trouble. Ideally, it would have been better to return gracefully to the womb and make another appearance – and to come out 'right' the next time around.

But times, styles, opinions and attitudes do change. We now know that black is and can be beautiful. Women can cornrow, plait, afro or straighten their hair if they like. What began as a political statement has settled into a comfortable, easy way to wear the hair; it gives black women a style all their own. The 'afro' became so popular that it moved out of the black community into the white community – a nice change. (The same thing happened to plaiting, which came to be known as the 'Bo Derek look'.)

Someone once compared a room full of black people to a garden of exotic flowers reflecting all the colours of a rainbow from cream to mahogany to ebony, but all nonetheless 'black'. Who would dare define a standard when we are a combination so unique as to defy any limiting description? Black is beautiful, black is joy, black is endless variety. In the 60s the designer Courrèges dedicated his short skirt to the Negro 'because black women have perfectly shaped knees'! Even today French designers are always eager to use black models.

We have tried in this book to set down some basic rules for skin care, hair care and make-up for the black woman of today: we feel she has been very neglected. We cannot be English roses; we are beautiful in our own right.

Barbara Jackson
1984

To Florence, my Mother

Lydia

To Jeanne Contini

Barbara

1 Skin

Your beautiful skin

Look carefully into the mirror at the mass covering your bones: it's called *SKIN*. It is perhaps the most important organ of your body; it is certainly the largest. It belongs to you for better or worse and reveals all of your bad habits: whether you smoke or drink, take birth control pills or eat greasy food. To be technical (look at the diagram on page 3 to help you understand), the top layer is called the *epidermis*. This layer is composed of dead cells layered like tiles on a roof, overlapping one another. They are waterproof, protect the inner layer and are replaced every day. On black skin they show up as those white 'ashy' bits we're all too familiar with.

Characteristics of black skin

The colour of black skin is determined by two things, the amount of *melanin* present in the cells, and the way in which light is reflected on the surface of the skin. White skin reflects light, while black skin absorbs light – how much depends on the amount of melanin in the cells. This magic ingredient protects black skin from the ultraviolet rays of the sun – obviously a preparation for life in a tropical climate. The degree and variety of skin colour throughout Africa, from the very blue-black of the Sudan to the light brown of East Africa, may reflect an adaptation of pigmentation related to the strength of the sun. In addition, this can protect black skin from many diseases, such as psoriasis and skin cancer. The epidermis of black skin is tougher than it is in white skin. Black skin also has a more generous supply of *sweat glands* ending in *pores*. Pores are larger in black skin than in white. Sweat, which is poured on to the skin from the pores, contains water and salts. Sweat gives the skin a sheen, often mistaken for and treated as 'oiliness'.

Moisture on the surface of the skin acts as a deterrent against ageing – a blessing in disguise, because it keeps the skin pliable and younger looking for longer. Black women usually don't begin to age until well after the age of fifty. It is important, though, to guard against blackheads and pimples, even in a light skin. Always cleanse your skin carefully.

'I never use anything on my face but soap and water. I LIKE the natural look.'

How often have you heard that statement repeated?
In an ideal world, with a moderate climate, no cold or very hot weather, no central heating (or chips), no air pollution, no chemicals in the air or in our food, and soft rainwater to drink and wash with (sheer bliss), it might be possible to have a skin soft as a baby's and to do absolutely nothing to keep it that way.

Albert Fornay, an expert in black cosmetics and skin care doesn't agree.
'I don't understand what people mean by "natural". We're not in the jungle – we live in a most unnatural environment, so you have to counteract chemical with chemical. I think it is ludicrous for a person to say they are natural; we all require some form of protection and hygienic routine for our bodies.'

We live in a real world and the skin of our face is the first line of defence against all types of wind and weather. Soap and water are fine – for a start. If you don't use a moisturiser,* you're asking for trouble for you are exposing your bare face to the elements. Make-up does serve the purpose of protecting the skin by providing a screen between it and the weather.
By now I hope we have convinced you that good skin doesn't just 'grow', it needs to be cultivated. It's not so much hard work as it sounds. First, determine what kind of skin you have, then learn to care for it. This can be done in a few minutes each day. It's true. Get yourself into a routine.

*See Chapter 3 *Make-up* for more information about all the cosmetics mentioned in this chapter.

The great divide

Skin is the outside covering of your body. It is waterproof, sensitive, supple, and elastic. Skin consists of two quite distinct layers. The outer layer or *epidermis* is constantly worn away and flakes off. These cells are continually replaced by new cells formed at the base of the epidermis. The deeper layer or *dermis* includes blood vessels, nerves, sweat glands and elastic tissues. Like all the organs in your body, skin is affected by diet. A balanced diet (see Chapter 4) ensures healthy skin. Because it's on the outside of your body skin is also subjected to a great deal of drying. Most skin creams act to re-moisturise the epidermis. Creams cannot penetrate the waterproof outer covering.

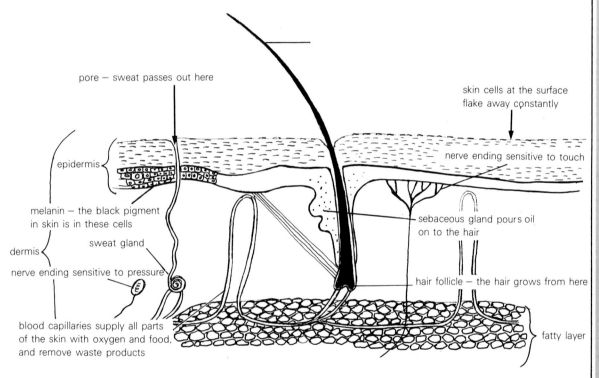

pore — sweat passes out here

skin cells at the surface flake away constantly

epidermis

nerve ending sensitive to touch

melanin — the black pigment in skin is in these cells

sebaceous gland pours oil on to the hair

dermis

sweat gland

nerve ending sensitive to pressure

hair follicle — the hair grows from here

blood capillaries supply all parts of the skin with oxygen and food, and remove waste products

fatty layer

Prevention is the wisest action in dealing with the inner layer, because treatment is almost impossible. Moisture and nutrients are supplied to this layer by your blood vessels, not by any cosmetics yet manufactured. There is no jelly, cream or ointment that can penetrate the dermis. If there was, it would probably do more harm than good. Damage to this layer can cause permanent scar tissue to form and affect the look of your face for years to come. At this stage, cosmetics cannot remedy, but only disguise harm done to this vital layer.

Which type are you?

Dry skin

Dry skin is more common in white people than in black people, due to the fact that black skin has a surfeit of sebaceous glands which supply the skin with oil. Examine your 'dry' skin carefully. If the skin on your face alone is dry while that on the rest of your body is normal, you should be a bit suspicious. It may be that you are exposing your face to some drying condition, like the harmattan wind or the central heating turned up too high; or perhaps you have an underactive thyroid or some other medical problem which is affecting your skin. Never forget that your skin mirrors your state of health.

Look at your skin again. If it's flaking and feels tight when you wash, it could be dry. In that case look to your diet or the conditions around you. Eat more oily fish, take cod liver oil pills and use a night cream before going to bed. Be sure to use a moisturiser during the day as well. Massage your skin, but don't pull or stretch it. Work out a beauty routine and stick to it! Wash your face with a superfatted or mild, unscented pure soap, followed by a non-alcoholic toner (preferably a flower water). Lastly, dab on your moisturiser while your face is still damp. If you fail to remove all traces of the cleanser and it dries on your face, you may end up with a worse problem. So don't be stingy with the water! Remember that moisturisers just keep the moisture in. Go easy on the night cream. Keep in mind that too much will clog already starved pores; and that skin will only absorb any cream for ten minutes. If your moisturiser contains urea, all the better, for it is a compound that attracts water to the skin and prevents its loss.

Your beauty routine begins when you get up.

Morning

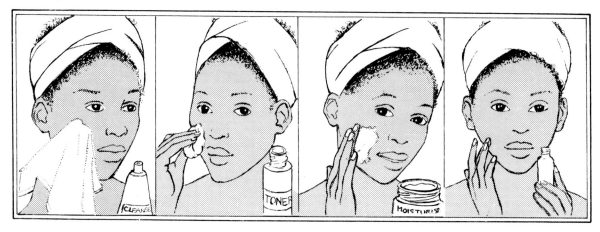

- Using a clean wash cloth, cleanse your face completely with a rinsable cleanser (or a water-soluble cleansing cream) and lukewarm water. This should take no more than sixty to ninety seconds.
- Use your toner to remove any traces of cleanser.
- Follow with an oil-based moisturiser. Allow it to dry. (This will take about ten minutes.)
- Apply your normal foundation.

Oily skin

When white skin has a shine, it's oily: when black skin shines it's probably natural.

You can see immediately whether you have oily skin or not. An oily skin is almost always just a bit shiny, especially around the nose and forehead. Blotting your face with a piece of tissue (the 'tissue' test) to determine whether your skin is oily or not, was developed with white skin in mind, skin with 'overworked sebaceous glands, sallow in colour and coarse in texture'! That doesn't describe black skin. We're not discouraging this test, but we do want you to be aware of its limitations.

Because many oil glands open directly on to the skin our skin may seem oily, when actually it's quite normal. In an effort to 'normalise' the skin, detergent cleansers are often used when they're not needed. It is true that black people who have lived away from Africa for three hundred years have acclimatised (they show less activity of the sebaceous glands); nevertheless, the sebum activity is still irrevocably connected to the genes. So black women must be careful not to go overboard in the use of cleansers and lotions termed 'for oily skin', especially if they contain acetone and have been developed with the white customer in mind. It is important to avoid removing too much oil from our skin – because it's natural.

Note: Readers in Africa should avoid using cosmetics and lotions packaged in plastic bottles because of the high risk of deterioration in very hot climates. If in doubt, keep everything in the fridge and be sure the jars and tubes are kept tightly closed.

Oily skin can sometimes be a blessing in disguise because it retains its resiliency longer than dry skin does. Sometimes it is also less prone to wrinkling. So when you're fighting to stave off those blackheads and the occasional skin problem aggravated by oiliness, just remember that oil protects and preserves!

The solution is cleansing – and more cleansing. Wash your face at least three times a day; take special care first thing in the morning and last thing at night. Wash! Wash! But beware of soap! Soap is good for floors and walls – but not always for faces. Use a cleansing lotion or baby oil to remove make-up, followed by an astringent for oily skins (alcohol is a bit too strong). Do be careful not to irritate the skin. If you feel that your face is not really clean without soap, use a mild anti-bacterial soap or a cleanser that rinses off with water. Does that sound clean enough for you?

Try to cleanse your skin with a lotion that is specially formulated for black skin. If one isn't available, then *READ* the labels carefully so that you can avoid anything that might cause your skin to dry out from over-cleansing. You could try a toner formulated for 'normal' white skin; it will do less damage. If you're not at all sure, try a flower lotion. We're not being cranky, just warning you that the 'wrong' cure may be worse than the original problem.

Do use a complexion brush or rough sponge for effective cleansing – but go easy with it, especially when using anti-bacteriological cleansers. Avoid creams with excessive amounts of glycerine or mineral oil; instead, opt for creams made from vegetable fats like groundnut or coconut.

Even though your skin is oily, you'll still need to use a moisturiser because oil-removing procedures used repeatedly can impair the moisture balance of your skin. Oil is one thing, moisture is quite another, so don't be over-enthusiastic to the point where you create another problem for yourself. The idea is to keep the skin clean and the pores healthy. To ward off black-heads use cleansing grains at least twice a week.

Very often, strong lotions and toners are recommended for an 'oily skin'; they're useful when used with care. As we said, try a toner formulated for 'normal' white skin if you're unable to find one made for black skin, or use a flower lotion. This is easily available at your local health store.

Now it's true that black people, because of their extra lashings of melanin, are less susceptible to allergies, but be on your guard! An indiscriminate use of lotions and cosmetics, all of which can deteriorate in the hot sun, can indeed cause irritation and damage to the skin.

Oily skin is sometimes thought to be synonymous with black-heads and pimples though I can hardly remember when I've seen an African person with a bad complexion. Move the African to a Western country and feed him (or her) on a diet high in animal fat and reconstituted food full of preservatives; add a lack of exercise, too much central heating, insufficient ventilation. Now you have a perfect formula for skin problems. But it doesn't have to be that way if you cleanse and tone. Don't strip the skin like an old chair in need of a repaint. Go easy on toners with a high alcohol content – you'll recognise them, they're the ones that make your eyes water – (have you ever seen your dad splashing on his after-shave?). Use witch-hazel or flower water, they're just as effective. Use a gentle cleansing lotion to remove make-up and remember to rinse it *ALL* off (no backsliding). Follow this with an astringent. If you like, you can choose a mild anti-bacterial soap or cleanser. Remember that oil is *not* moisture, so you will still need a mild, light moisturiser. (Baby lotion is very good.)

We have been conditioned to look for a 'matt finish' in cosmetics and are often willing to sacrifice a healthy natural sheen to obtain a finish which isn't at all natural!

Remember, black skin is naturally shiny, but not necessarily oily. So don't try to wash all the shine away; it's just telling us that our sebaceous glands are doing their job!

The routine (oily skin)

Your skin is going to look better, longer, if you take care of it and enjoy it! Treat it lovingly. Cleanse, tone and moisturise. Does that sound familiar?

Skip the moisturiser at night, except for under the eyes, where there are no oil glands.

Morning

- *Cleanse* Always use a clean face cloth.

  Try using a medicated skin cream under make-up; it's an excellent non-greasy moisturiser for oily skin.

  Massage gently; don't pull.

  If you do use an anti-bacterial soap, don't use it *every* day, it's like using a sledge-hammer to crack a nut. In the same way as using an anti-dandruff shampoo every time can dry out your hair, you may end up with dry skin!! The one exception to this rule is if you have bad acne.

- *Tone*   Use a toner/freshener. Pat it on with a clean wad of cotton wool (not around your eyes).
- *Moisturise*   Smooth on a water-based moisturiser for oily skin. Wait ten minutes, then blot off any excess.
Apply your foundation.

Night

No matter *HOW* tired you are, *ALWAYS* remove all your make-up before going to bed. Learn to do it quickly so that you can't use the excuse of being 'too tired'.

- *Cleanse*   This time use a rough sponge (though *not* around the eyes), perhaps wrung out in some high-class liquid soap. Lovely!
- *Rinse*   Rinse again . . . Pat dry.
- *Moisturise*   Use a light moisturiser and always stroke it on upwards, starting at the chin. Use your middle finger to avoid applying too much pressure. Black skin also responds to *dry* massage if it is especially oily. This helps push oil out of the pores.

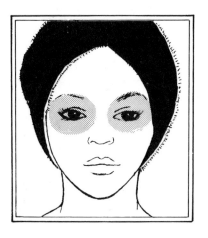

Masks

You can safely give yourself a facial every ten days – unless you happen to have very oily, blemished skin. In that case a weekly facial is a must.
Assemble everything you need in the bathroom first.
Of course you can buy a mask, but the ones you make at home are cheaper – and better. Fuller's earth and oatmeal are two things you should *always* have in the house. Buy a quantity of oatmeal from your local health shop and keep it in the bathroom in a nice large jar.

Oatmeal face scrubs

- Mix enough oatmeal with water to make a paste. Put it on your face and let it dry for ten to fifteen minutes. Wash it off. Simple, right?
- Mix 2 teaspoonsful of oatmeal together with 1 tablespoonful of almond meal until you have a paste. Use as above.
Mix 1 tablespoonful each of oatmeal and fuller's earth. Add a splash of witch-hazel, (or the juice of half a lemon) and a table-spoonful of cleansing cream. Use immediately. Leave the mask on for fifteen minutes. Remove it with lukewarm water.

Astringent

- Make your own astringent by mixing 1 teaspoonful of lemon juice with 2 tablespoonsful of water, OR one part of witch-hazel with 2 parts of rosewater.
- Of course you can purchase an over-the-counter peeling agent – which is especially good for black skin.
- Invest in a good, soft, complexion brush.
- Try a 'revitalising clay' mask.

This quest for better looking skin is certainly not new! Today women have vast quantities of creams, oils, emulsions and the like to beautify their skin; women in seventeenth century England were so keen to keep their complexions beautiful that they wore masks outdoors – and sometimes indoors as well!

Normal skin

– lucky you!

Maybe you're lucky enough to have what is termed a 'normal' skin. It will have little shine, the pores will be hardly visible, you will have no lines, blackheads or pimples. It is clear and smooth and the envy of all your friends. It is flawless. For a black person this 'normal' skin may just be slightly oily, soft and smooth to the touch. It is just the type of skin we are trying to persuade our readers to achieve! If you look around you, you will see many black skins that are normal, devoid of make-up and have the texture of velvet. Lucky girl if this describes you. Cleanse and moisturise your 'normal' skin and stay away from heavy make-up. But do not take it for granted, because pregnancy or just the fact of growing up or growing older may change it. You should cleanse with a mild soap and finish with a light moisturiser for protection.

Combination skin

This is what most of us have. It is usually oily in the 'T'-zone (forehead, nose and chin), and somewhat dryer on the cheeks and throat and round the eyes. How dry is relative. Do treat the 'oily' T-zone as for oily skin – but not with anything that will strip the skin completely. Use a mild skin freshener. Cleanse with a complexion brush and complexion soap. Use a light moisturiser. If the combination is 'oily' and 'more oily', then use an astringent to control your shine, and keep away from heavy make-up that will clog the pores. You could try one of the new formulas for black skin that are available now.

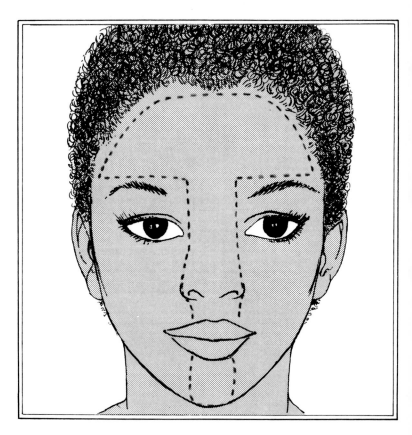

- *Cleanse* morning and evening to remove make-up. Use either a mild liquid cleanser or a water-soluble cream. Use an astringent on your T-zone, and flower water on your cheeks and throat.

- *Blot* your T-zone before applying foundation.
  In the evening you might try massaging your face gently with dry fingers for a few minutes. Then break open a capsule of vitamin E and, using a Q-tip, spread it under your eyes.
- *Never* use a deodorant soap on your face.
- *Never* use soap that everybody else uses to wash their hands.
- *Always* use a clean face cloth or cotton wool for cleansing.
- *Never* touch your face unless you've first washed your hands.

Treat yourself

You have, at your fingertips, a myriad of cleansers, toners and applications for every part of the skin. You can slather yourself with potions offered by all of the cosmetics houses – most of them are useful and convenient and by all means help yourself. But if you would like to try something new – or strange – visit your local health store. If you live in or are visiting London, pay a visit to one of the many apothecary stores – especially if you're not in the mood to mix and mix at home. They have a fascinating collection of cleansers, moisturisers, shampoos, herbs and ointments that are natural and excellent for the skin. The criterion is, I think, if you can eat it, at least it's not bad for your skin. Read on . . .

Cleansers   Sage and elderflower: These are good for problem and oily skins. Sage is stimulating and elderflower is most soothing.

Moisturisers   Yarrow and comfrey: These are very light and slightly astringent. Allantoin, which is used in many cosmetics, is derived from comfrey. It is popular for its healing and cell-regenerating properties.

Toners   Choose from witch-hazel, orangeflower water or rosewater.

Teen skin

Being a teenager is something that most of us have lived through and gone on to fight another day. It's a time when marauding hormones can produce havoc in our lives, causing spots and greasy skin just when we want to be appealing to the opposite sex. We want to know everything and sometimes feel that everbody knows more than we do – especially about things that affect us most. Being a teenager can be demanding: aside from the changes going on in our bodies, we are often facing decisions at school about the future. Adults, especially, seem smug and/or busy and people over twenty-five seem ancient! To add insult to injury your body is producing nothing but surprises all the time. What next?

Of course, you can escape teen acne; some teenagers exhibit none of the symptoms at all and just have to handle the emotional problems of feeling very adult one day and absolutely childlike the next.

If you learn how to care for your skin, there will be one less thing to plague you.

Teen skin isn't all acne and horrors, but it still needs care. There is no better time to learn how to begin to care for your skin for the rest of your life. Get ready now for those times when you will be busy working, or raising a family, or both, and won't have time to indulge in long drawn out beauty routines. So, learn now when you have time to fool around.

Acne

This can be the plague of teenage life. It's a natural process that many, if not all young people go through. Acne isn't a disease, it's simply a condition caused by the new activity of sex hormones and diet. The chief manifestation of this condition is the ever present (or threatening to be) blackhead. When the sac-like sebaceous gland gets blocked by dirt and grease, it thickens at the opening and turns black, white or brown as it meets the air. Behold! a blackhead, and most times more than just one! Acne is *not* terminal; if blocked or infected pores are treated, there should be no scarring. Trouble may occur, in rare cases, when the infection travels down and begins to attack the under layer of the skin, causing deep scarring. This is rare in black skin despite the fact that black people have many more oil glands than do white people. It seems that the excess production of oil is counteracted by an equally abundant production of oestrogenic secretion. (Oestrogen is the female hormone.)

Nonetheless, if you do happen to suffer badly from acne, it can be treated by cleansing (morning and evening) with the relevant soaps and the application of a medicated lotion. We often use the term 'thinning' here; it just means to remove the top layer of dead cells (particularly important for acne sufferers), excess oil and dirt. Sea salt is good for this. Use a clean wash cloth wrung out in warm water (slightly wet). Sprinkle on salt and rub gently using a circular motion over the cheeks, forehead and chin. Use a horizontal motion on the nose, sides of the face and neck. This treatment is best carried out at night so that the skin has a chance to relax. If you continue this treatment for two minutes, three times a week, it should relieve your acne. Always cleanse first. It's all right to use soap once a week, but we wouldn't recommend more than that. It's all right to use a liquid cleanser as long as you rinse it *all* off. Always blot your face dry with a clean towel after washing it.

Make-up

If you are using make-up, use a water-based foundation, but never try to hide acne scars with thick make-up. Do not squeeze pimples or blackheads; you may cause blemishes or deep scarring if you do.

By now, if you have been reading carefully, you will know that the skin grows up and out – if you give it half a chance. It consists of several layers of cells with nerves and blood vessels at the bottom which feed the skin and make it healthy (or unhealthy). Skin 'sheds' every day, and it is important to wash away this top layer of dead cells with soap, lotion, beauty grains or a cream with an abrasive action.

If you must use soap, use one of the white, unscented bars on the market; the purer the soap the less the alkali. Remember the ring in the bath tub? It is not caused by water! As black skin, because of its sebaceous gland make-up, already deposits a somewhat alkaline residue on the skin, it is not desirable to increase this by using a soap high in alkaline. It just takes more effort to remove it – twenty to thirty rinsings with very hot water! If you must use soap, use one that is pure and non-alkaline.

You must see that your skin gets a sufficient amount of oxygen (from the air) so do not use anything that clogs up your pores. You already have melanin to protect you from seventy-five per cent of the sun's ultraviolet rays, so you are well away, but do not expect too many miracles if you are not prepared at least to help out a bit. How?

Never go to bed without first cleansing your face with a cleansing cream or lotion. Wipe or 'tissue' off completely with a crumpled nappy liner (softer than tissues). Wipe clean with a mild toner and then apply a light moisturiser. That's all, except – a warning: don't wait until you have the odd blackhead to rush around trying to clean up a neglected skin, the way you'd clean up a neglected house if you suddenly found that a guest was downstairs. Do a bit every day. Get your routine right – and keep it for the rest of your life. You won't regret it.

Three facials for you

First cleanse your face thoroughly and dry it.

- You will need the following: camomile, peppermint, marigold flowers and burdock. Wash an unbreakable bowl and place the herbs in it. Cover with boiling water (as you would tea leaves), and leave for twenty minutes. You could do this the day before. Then strain and use what you need. Place the remainder in a tightly sealed glass container – for next time.

You will need the following: sage, yarrow and camomile. Mix together and use as above.

Mix together: 2 teaspoonsful of witch-hazel and 1 teaspoonful of dried yeast.

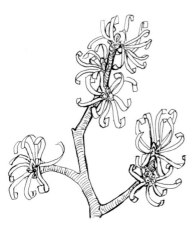

Mature skin

'Women don't get older, they get better!'
Whoever said that was absolutely right.

I've seen black women who are 'mature', have grown-up children, have worked every day of their lives and, if it's possible, look even better in their forties and fifties than they did when they were young(er). Of course the presence of melanin and that extra sebum does help. Obviously, the skin does change as we get older, but not so much from age as from neglect.

A little preservation goes a long way. A bit of moisturiser can stave off the wrinkles and dryness that one 'naturally' associates with growing older. We have said it before: your skin will tell on you when everyone else is being quiet.

Your metabolism tends to slow down somewhat as the years go by, and there may be changes in your skin. Cosmetic firms would have us believe that the magic age is thirty. Black skin does not begin to age this early. There may sometimes be a cellular build-up – maybe yes, maybe no. It depends on the care you have taken of your skin and on your lifestyle – or it may just depend on how wisely you've chosen your ancestors. Heredity plays a very big part in the ageing process (in black and white people). But that doesn't mean that you can just abandon *any* and all skin care. Remember – a little prevention will help a lot. Melanin will stave off those 'laugh lines' for a long time, but don't forget that the central heating, drying winds and the acid rain in the atmosphere are not our friends. If your skin begins to feel a bit 'thickish' and loses its tone, try thinning. This just means removing the tough outer layer with some gritty substance like

sea salt. It will give the new cells a chance to reach the surface. Try using a rough sponge, it is very effective. After using it, moisturise lightly. Don't pay as much attention to the date on your birth certificate as to how your skin looks in the mirror and feels to the touch.

For 'sloughing' you need beauty grains or 'scrubs'. Be sure to rinse well after using. Give soap a miss, it leaves an alkaline residue on the skin which is extremely difficult to remove. You could try a 'peeling' mask.

There is not, as yet, a heavy demand from black women for any of the 'miracle' creams which penetrate down into the sub-cutaneous layer of the skin and act to correct skin problems and speed up cell regeneration. There may be some interest in these preparations which 'restore' the skin's cellular metabolism to a 'younger level', or promote 'cell renewal' or contain 'collagen breakdown'. Collagen is a word you'll see often in magazines advertising cosmetics or 'skin rejuvenators' for older women. Collagen is the protein found in bones, tendons and under the skin where it is part of the elastic tissue support of the skin. Some doctors contend that the collagen used in cosmetics serves no useful purpose as it cannot penetrate down through the layers.

For black skin, the use of coconut oil or, even better, cocoa butter is recommended. Both of these are easily obtainable today, and black women from the Caribbean will be very familiar with their emollient and healing attributes.

Fade creams, etc (commonly and erroneously called bleach creams)

As a result of her wish to have a complexion that is suitable for cosmetics, the black women has long been known to use fade creams. Fade creams, by law, all contain the same amount of hydroquinone (approximately 2%). Hydroquinone is water-soluble. It works by inhibiting the production of melanin when placed on the skin. It evens out the complexion to make the face more receptive to cosmetics, and should not be worn in the sun, unless directed. Fade creams now come with vitamin E, or you can add your own vitamin E as you use the cream. Vitamin E is good for the skin.

Treat yourself

Dry skin

Cleanser Calendula – 'combines the soothing and cleansing qualities from marigolds'. Wow!

Moisturiser Almond – combines the nourishing and moisturising qualities of almond oil, beeswax and rosewater – good for dry and sensitive skin.

Normal skin

Cleanser Camomile – 'combines cleansing powers of camomile flower with a balanced cleanser ideally suited for normal skin'.

Moisturiser Marshmallow – just imagine – a mixture of oils and beeswax combined with the softening properties extracted from marshmallow root to make a perfect moisturiser.

17

HELP!

Problems?   Well, nobody's perfect

Human beings are extremely adaptable. Just look at us, we've been hauled all around the world, exposed to various climates, lived under stressful conditions (to say the least), and all the time those little melanocytes have been working (like the duck's busy little feet – paddling all the time) to protect us from most of the changes we've been subjected to. We have hair to protect the skull in tropical heat, skin that screens out the burning ultraviolet rays of the sun, the sickle cell to help protect us from malaria. While we may have a built-in protection against the worst ravages of acne, there are skin problems which have continued to puzzle doctors treating black patients.

Vitiligo – which 'shows' itself as the loss of pigment in large (or small) areas of the skin – still baffles doctors. It also affects white people but, of course, it is not as noticeable on a white skin as it is on a black skin. So far no 'cure' has been found, so the only thing that sufferers can do is try to disguise the paler areas.
Adele Davis, in her book *Let's Get Well* (page 115) suggests that this may be a symptom of malnutrition of a sort. She advises increasing the liver intake of your diet to 150 to 300 milligrams of pantothenic acid or 1000 milligrams of PABA, daily.
A new corrective cosmetic has just come on to the market and is useful in concealing the depigmented areas. It should be available at your local chemist in eight shades.

Keloid scars are familiar to every black person who has had an operation, a deep cut or a gash. All the protection afforded by having thick skin works against the black patient in this case simply because scar tissue regenerates at such a rapid pace that keloid tissue is formed. This is peculiar to black skin; though white people living in the tropics can develop keloids, they are likely to heal naturally when they return to a cooler climate. With black people this is not the case. We tend to develop keloids wherever we live. In recent times, doctors have had some success in preventing keloids by treating the scar with hydrocortisone.
Could there be a vitamin cure? Perhaps. Some success has been achieved by giving the patient 1200 milligrams of vitamin E until the discomfort of the keloid is relieved. 'Can it be,' asks Adele Davis (*Let's Get Well*, page 30), 'that coloured people have an unusually high requirement for vitamin E, which causes them to form scar tissue more readily than those of other races?' It's an interesting theory.

Stretch marks worry all women, but again they take on larger and more serious proportions when endured by a black woman. There are many folk cures which we won't go into, but again Adele Davis in her book *Let's Get Well* (page 114) claims that some relief can be had by 'staying on a high protein diet, supplemented with 600 units of vitamin E and 300 milligrams of pantothenic acid daily'.

You've already met comfrey or its deritive allantoin, known for its cell regenerative attributes. Comfrey and goldenseal infused and applied to stretch marks is a sure cure or so my relatives from the deep south of the United States tell me. *OR*: Comfrey, together with vitamin E cream may also work. It's worth a try. Any of the above are also good for acne scars.

Sensitive skin?

That means that you will always have to guard against any skin care or cosmetic preparations containing perfumes or additives of any kind – anything, in fact, that might set your skin on the path of eruption, spots or rashes. For cleansing, always use a soft soap – that is a glycerin or transparent soap. It will be kind to your skin.

- Read every label carefully; one word to look out for is 'hypo-allergenic'.
- When in doubt try baby lotions and soaps: they are usually inexpensive and as light as the proverbial feather. Baby oil is very good for removing make-up.
- Witch-hazel (undiluted) is excellent as an astringent.

Come clean

(It all began with water ...)

'After the age of twenty-five you're responsible for your own face.'

WRONG. It begins a lot earlier – with washing.

A quick lick and a promise is all right for the very young, they have time to learn, but if you want a beautiful complexion, free from excess oil, clear, with a nice texture, you'll have to learn how to wash your face properly.

Getting your face half clean is no trouble at all; getting it really clean needn't be a chore. Here's how you should go about it:

First of all *never* use hot water on your face. Use a mild soap or a liquid cleanser that will get off all the make-up and grime.

There are countless products on the market for you to choose from, many specially developed for deep cleansing. There are medicated soaps and cleansing grains for oily skins; lotions and creams for normal skins; superfatted soap for dry skins: liquids and aerosol foams. Many contain antiseptics for disturbed skins; one even contains camphor to cool your skin! Take your choice, follow the directions given, and be sure to select the right one for your skin type. Remember, the things you put on your face while washing it are simply to help the water to remove make-up and dirt. Your object is to wash, quickly and efficiently.

How?

Tie your hair back with a scarf.
Have a clean face flannel ready.

- Wet face with lots of lukewarm water.
- Work cleanser, soap or liquid gently into the skin, using a circular motion, covering your face and neck.
- Complete cleansing in not more than a minute and a half.
- Rinse thoroughly again with lukewarm water to remove *all* traces of the cleanser.

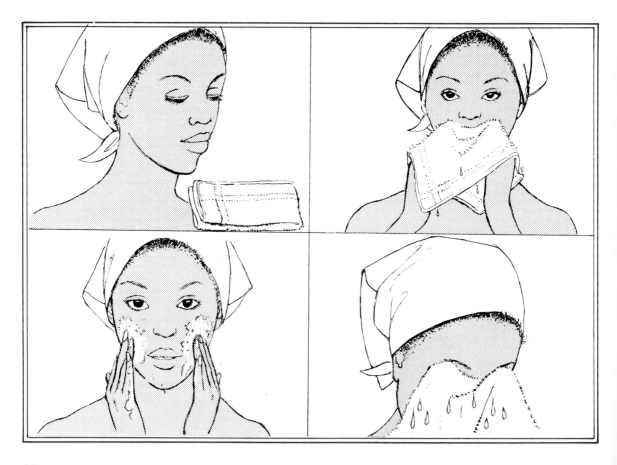

Save your dreaming time for the rinsing, not the cleansing. Your cleanser should fulfil several functions to complete its job which is to

- remove make-up/dirt thoroughly.
- be non-irritating.
- be easily and completely removed itself.

Moisturisers . . .
Toners . . .
Fresheners . . .
Astringents . . .

What are they and what do they do?

Do they really moisturise? By depositing a thin layer on the skin, they help to keep the skin's natural moisture in. If they do that job well, then they're successful. The best kind of moisturising still comes from within. I won't include another of those drawings resembling a piece of hairy sponge (look at page 3), but I will remind you that the inner layer of skin works all the time; one of its jobs is to keep the face in shape. It is difficult, almost impossible in fact, to repair any damage done to this layer – though some people in the beauty business maintain that recent findings 'prove' that certain specially formulated creams do have the ability to penetrate the top layer and enter the blood stream. Vitamin creams applied to the surface of the skin have been known to show 'some' success. We cannot add to or solve this controversy, but will simply warn women to think seriously about using *any* cream or lotion which alters the skin's metabolism (chemical changes that occur in the skin) and affects the function of the (inner) or sub-cutaneous layer of the skin.
Moisturisers, at best, fight a delaying action. They

- help the skin to maintain its water balance.
- help protect the skin from pollution.
- help to make the texture of the skin soft.
Night creams will be even more effective if you first cover your face with a wet cloth, for a few minutes.
Tinted moisturisers are not particularly good for the skin, because of the chemicals used in the pigments and the powders used to produce these products. Our advice is that a tinted moisturiser should be applied *over* your moisturiser.

Now that your skin is clean, mop up and remove all traces of cleanser/soap with a toner, a freshener, or an astringent. It can be confusing because of the jargon that has grown up around these words, sometimes describing the same thing in different terms, and using expressions that have little to do with what the product actually does. These products should finally clean the face and leave it ready for a moisturiser. That's it! Witch-hazel will very often do this job, diluted of course.

Many of these products contain alcohol, especially those formulated for the mature skin. These have deep cleansing properties. We do not recommend you to use alcohol-based cleansers too often, if at all, as they, in turn, can dry out the skin too much. They are however, excellent for a quick cleanse of the pores. The addition of fruit or vegetable substances (usually artificial) to toners, etc is of little benefit. If your toner, freshener or astringent claims to be practically a wonder drug, be suspicious. It may have too many ingredients to be of any positive help. Many of these products act like a thin liquid soap – and that's it. Lubricants and humectants (moisteners) are often added to make the toner feel smooth. Psychologically, that's all right, because it makes you feel better, but it doesn't mean that they benefit the skin.

If a freshener has a high alcohol content, then it will be described as an 'astringent'.

A skin freshener, in the most basic terms, can be a pleasant smelling and smoothing concoction, which makes the skin feel clean – much the same as an after-shave lotion!

You may need a guide through the 'cleanser' maze of definitions. A cleanser low in oils (suitable for oily skin) is termed a 'milk'. One high in oil content is called a 'cream/creme'. An 'emulsion' is somewhere between the two, with a composition of lighter oils, suspended in differing amounts of water. Soapless cleansers are a form of liquid soap – helpful for cleansing blemished skin.

Moisturisers – which one?

Probably in the year 2000 doctors and cosmeticians will still be debating the benefits of and necessity for moisturisers – showing that we still don't know as much about the skin as we might. The function of a moisturiser is to keep the moisture, which is directed up from the inner layer, from escaping. Believe it or not, H_2O – yes, water – is the best moisturiser.

Baths

You don't have to be a Roman emperor or Cleopatra to have a glamorous bath. It's yours for the asking. But you do have to know how to have a bath which is beneficial for your skin, and which won't leave your skin clogged with a heavy, oily, scented film.

Baths are primarily for cleaning the skin. If you want to soak, that's fine, but don't soap and soak at the same time. Sitting in a tub full of hot, soapy, alkaline water isn't particularly beneficial to your skin. Fill the tub with water – not too hot, if you please. You can either soap and rinse at the beginning, or at the end, but soap and rinse you must. Then soak if you please, especially if your poor old bones are tired, or you just want to relax.

You might put a cupful or two of Epsom salts into the water; it's relaxing and also softens the water. This is especially useful if you live in the south-east of Britain, or any other hard-water area.

Is your skin irritated or blemished? Put a handful of bicarbonate of soda in your bath water.

Sea salt, which you can buy quite easily, will soothe muscles flagged out from a day of shopping; a tablespoonful will do nicely.

Camomile is relaxing and sleep-inducing and has been around for as long as we have thought of such things. Make an infusion, or use some ready-made tea bags, which should be available from your health store.

Oatmeal (would you believe?) should be a household standby. It is a good water softener: tie some up in a piece of cheesecloth and put it in the bath water.

If your cupboard is really bare, try some household starch. Mix it up with a little water in a small container and pour it into your bath water as you run the tap. It's especially good if you've 'reached the end of your rope' and the kids have been howling all day!

These are just a few of the bath additives which you have at your disposal twelve months of the year. We're not saying that you shouldn't use any of those lovely, sweet-smelling, bottled gifts you've received; we're just trying to explain what they do (and don't do) to your skin.

Have a go at making your own bath oil by combining a quarter of a teaspoonful of any of the essential oils (lavender, almond, sandalwood, lemon, patchouli or orange) with 2 tablespoonsful of liquid detergent and half a cup of safflower, peanut or seasame oil.

Do read the label and be sure, if you do buy a bath oil, that it's a dispersing one that percolates through the water and silkens your skin as you bath rather than just floating on the top of the water in a greasy oil slick.

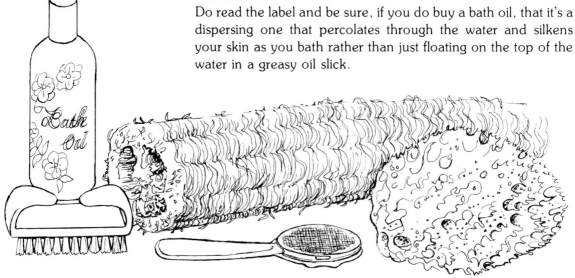

Treat yourself to a loofah – they come in various forms such as mitts and in an oblong, netlike shape.

Once you're out of the tub pat yourself dry and apply a body lotion, and a splash of cologne, which is better applied when your body is still warm. Finish with some talcum powder.

Never use deodorant soap on your face, or use the same wash cloth on your face that you use on your body.

Going out for the evening? Spray on cologne or perfume (lightly) before dressing. Never spray them on your clothes.

Don't neglect your feet. Give yourself a pedicure.

Deodorants

Everyone needs a deodorant. Perspiration in itself is not unpleasant, it's just when it combines with the air that it develops an unpleasant odour. A deodorant will simply remove the odour, while not preventing perspiration. If you perspire heavily, then it may be wise to use an anti-perspirant which will help to inhibit perspiration. It is not unhealthy to use an anti-perspirant as the sweat will find its way out of your body in other ways.

However, as stale perspiration can be unpleasant, and ruinous to clothes, it is advisable to use whichever cream or lotion is most suitable – unless you have unlimited amounts of money to keep replacing clothes ruined when the armpits drop out! Years ago, when most clothes were made of natural fibres like wool or cotton, it was unnecessary to use the amount of prevention we need today. As most of today's clothes are manufactured from man-made fibres (nylon, viscose, terylene, etc) they do not 'breathe', and so hold in the perspiration – and the odour.

Depilatories

Do use a depilatory to remove the hair from under your arms unless you prefer to shave. Whichever method you use, do wait twenty-four hours before using a deodorant. Use cologne instead. Always use a bit of talcum powder after you have applied your daily deodorant.

Remember, it's difficult for your deodorant to work properly if you have hair under your arms.

Masks

– all dressed up and ready for fun!

Well, not quite, we are just going to have our weekly face mask. Facials are not anything new; women have been covering their faces with skin-preserving substances for centuries, hoping that their skin would be sparkling and firm when they removed whatever the substance was. It is a bit easier today because we can, if we wish, purchase a workable face mask in our local chemist shop, or, if we are just a bit adventurous, we could make our own.

To the rescue

Facials are a great help in the face-saving department. There are all kinds of masks on the market which do different things to the skin. Some tighten pores, some absorb oil or moisture. Facial masks come in three different types.

Soothing masks, excellent for mature skins, temporarily contract pores and eliminate the graininess caused by dry skin. Our ancestors living on the banks of the Nile quickly learned the benefits of the clay mask for restoring and rejuvenating the skin. From that time to this, women have travelled to health spas for these benefits.

Like most other skin preparations, facials and masks do not work miracles for hopeless skin. When used regularly, however,

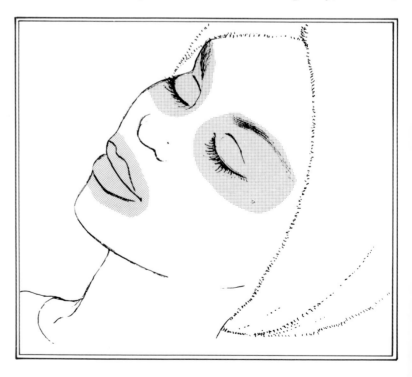

they can refine the skin, stimulate circulation, unclog pores and carry away the impurities that have accumulated.

Stimulating masks make the skin sparkle and feel young by speeding up circulation. Some are mentholated and soothing, others have bracing ingredients that firm contours and tighten pores for a time.

Medicated masks are good for lifeless or disturbed skins, not only for teens, but for all ages.

Some of these stay on for half an hour, and others for just five minutes.

Choose the correct one for your skin type, and have fun – they make your face feel like new!

There are store-bought facials and home-made ones. Have you got cucumbers, honey, mayonnaise, eggs, beet juice? The makings of a salad, yes, but also the ingredients that go into facials that you can put together yourself from your refrigerator shelves. Long before the advent of the corner chemist, women were concocting ways to make their complexions beautiful to see and touch. Many of these 'secrets' found their way to women all the way down to the present time. Whether you've found oatmeal edible or not, remember that it is excellent to wear because of its tightening and smoothing properties.

Recipes

- Egg white with honey: Beat the egg white until it's stiff. Stir in a teaspoonful of honey before you fluff the mixture on your face. It is a bit sticky, but great for tightening the pores. Just don't do it in a room full of cotton wool!
- For puffiness of the face, use the white of an egg (slightly beaten). Spread it on the face and neck for five minutes, wash off with cool water. This is also excellent for bruises.
- Mix raw oatmeal with enough buttermilk to make a paste, or you can mash oatmeal with grated cucumber until the cucumber juice moistens it enough to make it stick to your face. Spread it on, let it dry for fifteen minutes and then rinse it off.

Choose a mask for your own particular needs and skin type: dry; oily; combination; all-purpose; treatment of blemished skin. A weekly mask is also a morale booster, especially if your youthful skin is troubled with blemishes or blackheads. You might wish to steam your face, but you don't have to. You can, of course, steam on your own. Steaming will help open the pores and prepare your face for a more deep cleansing. For dry or mature skin, leave the mask on for ten to twenty minutes, removing it just before it gets too hard. For oily skins leave it on until it sets, in about fifteen minutes. Masks come in 'wash off' or 'peel off' varieties.

Masks (for one and all)

- Smooth on a light layer of cream, stroking upwards from the throat. Pour some boiling water into a bowl. Use herbs if you like (elder flowers or sage are good for a dry skin). Drape a towel over your head and bend over a bowl for six to eight minutes.
- Apply the mask according to directions. Do not put it around the eyes. Here you should apply some moisturising cream or vaseline. Lie down and relax until it's time to remove the mask. Once a month is often enough for sensitive skins.

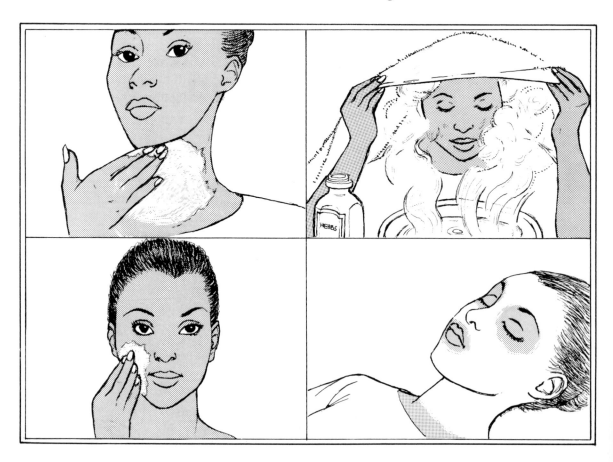

Recipes

- Mix 1 egg yolk with a tablespoon of pure, strained honey. Smooth the mixture on your neck and face, lie down and relax for fifteen minutes. Remove mask with a towel dipped in lukewarm water.
- Melt a teaspoonful of sweet butter and mix it with 2 table-spoonsful of whole fresh milk. Apply to the face and leave it on for fifteen minutes. Wash the mask off as above.
- Mix together a whole beaten egg, 1 tablespoonful of fresh milk and half a teaspoonful of honey until they have a creamy consistency.
- Cocoa butter is excellent as a moisturiser and can be used over the entire body. It nourishes and protects the skin and gives it a nice sheen.
- Mayonnaise is an excellent cleanser for dry skin. Believe it!
- Cleanse with a pure liquid soap.

Face packs (combination skin)

Of course you can buy one ready made! But that's not half so much fun as a home-made face pack; besides, you'll never have a face pack that's so fresh.

- Don't mix the white of an egg with anything – just beat it and put it on your face!
- Combine 1 tablespoonful of brewer's yeast with half a teaspoonful of wheat germ oil. Mix in enough *hot* milk to make a paste and spread it on with *easy* strokes. Leave it on for twenty minutes. Remove with lukewarm water.
- Got some yoghurt you haven't eaten? Combine 1 tablespoonful with 1 tablespoonful of fuller's earth and add a teaspoonful of mint. Leave it on for fifteen minutes. Rinse with cool water.

Assemble everything you need:
1   Mask (your own or store bought).
2   A wooden spoon for mixing.
3   Moisturiser for your eyes/mouth.
4   Towel for cleaning your face.
5   Cleanser.
6   Witch-hazel (for toning afterwards if you are going to apply make-up). You can alternatively wring the cotton wool out in witch-hazel and place the pads over your eyes.
7   Night cream if you're going to bed.
Only apply a mask on a very, very clean face. Use your own brand of cleanser — or make your own.

Deep cleansing

Mix together
- 2 tablespoonsful of oatmeal with enough water to make a paste.
- 2 tablespoonsful of oatmeal with 1 tablespoonful of ground almonds. Add enough water to make a paste.

Steaming

Steaming is extremely effective if used in conjunction with a cleansing mask. Assemble everything you need:
1   A towel to drape over your head.
2   A bowl of hot water.
3   Some herbs to add if you like (be a devil!) — just a handful is enough.

Wheat germ softening mask

Mix 1 tablespoonful of dry brewer's yeast with half a teaspoonful of wheat germ oil. Add enough fresh milk to make a paste. Spread the mixture on your face. Leave it for twenty minutes. Rinse with lukewarm water.

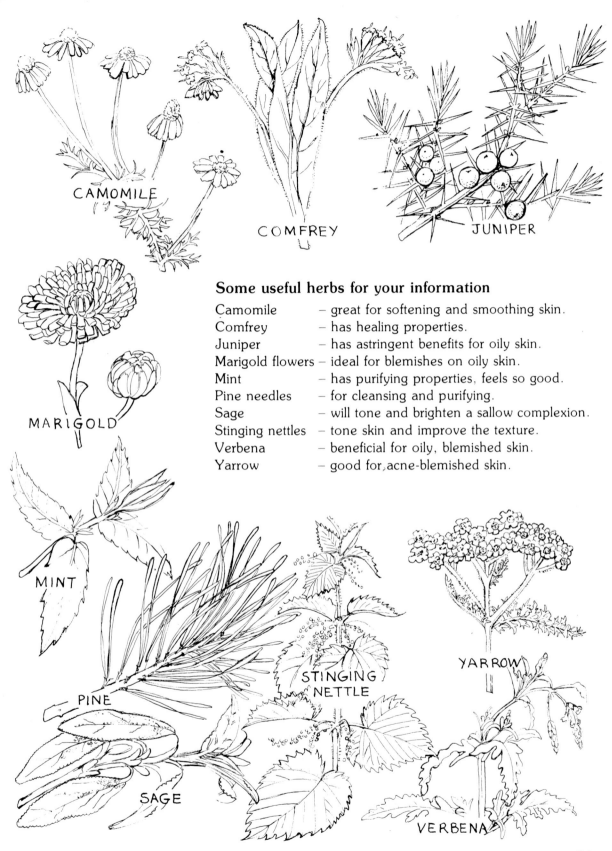

CAMOMILE

COMFREY

JUNIPER

MARIGOLD

Some useful herbs for your information

Camomile	– great for softening and smoothing skin.
Comfrey	– has healing properties.
Juniper	– has astringent benefits for oily skin.
Marigold flowers	– ideal for blemishes on oily skin.
Mint	– has purifying properties, feels so good.
Pine needles	– for cleansing and purifying.
Sage	– will tone and brighten a sallow complexion.
Stinging nettles	– tone skin and improve the texture.
Verbena	– beneficial for oily, blemished skin.
Yarrow	– good for acne-blemished skin.

MINT

PINE

STINGING NETTLE

YARROW

SAGE

VERBENA

Helpful hints

Petroleum jelly	For removing eye make-up.
Cucumbers	Slices for tired eyes.
Oatmeal + water	Make into a paste for scrubbing oily skin.
Avocado	Use as a moisturiser for dry skin.
Honey	Use as a facial mask ($\frac{1}{2}$ lemon and 1 teaspoonful of honey).
Lemon juice	Lightens dark spots.
Mayonnaise	Good for dry skin and hair.
Prevention and cure for blackheads	Mix a teaspoonful of cornmeal and a teaspoonful of cleansing cream together. Gently massage into skin, paying close attention to chin and nose. Tissue off and rinse with warm water.
Remedy for minor skin blemishes, clogged pores	Mix equal amounts of sea salt and hand cream or moisturising cream and gently massage using a circular motion. Rinse with warm water. Apply moisturiser.
Last minute facial before a big night	Mix honey and egg white. Cover face and leave it on for five minutes, until dry. Rinse off with warm water.
Remove freckles or lighten dark areas	Mix $\frac{1}{2}$ teaspoonful of lemon juice with $\frac{1}{2}$ teaspoonful of baby oil.
Teeth	Brush with equal amounts of baking soda and table salt.

Dry, sensitive 'winter' skin	To a half-full tub of warm water, add 1 cup powdered milk, ½ cup of salt and ½ cup of baby oil.
Irritated skin	Add a handful of laundry starch (that's right!) to a half-full tub of warm water.
Had a hard day?	Add 2 cups of Epsom salts to your bath.
Rough elbows?	Squeeze ½ lemon, add a few drops of baby oil. Cut a lemon in half, squeeze out the juice and sit with elbows in the lemon cups for a few minutes.
Rough nails?	Immerse in a combination of honey and orange juice for ten minutes. Rinse.
Slices of potatoes on eyes	Useful when you give yourself a facial.
Tired, calloused feet?	Heat some olive oil and rub it into your feet. Sleep in a pair of cotton socks. For tougher skin, rub with pumice stone.
Rough winter hands?	Put lots of moisturiser on your hands at night and slip on a pair of white cotton gloves.
Puffy eyes?	After you have wrung out wads of cotton wool in cold water, repeat with witch-hazel and apply to your eyes for fifteen minutes.
	Mix some comfrey (available at health shops) into a powder and combine with some water. Soak 2 wads of cotton wool and place over your eyes.

2 Hair

Crowning glory – or crown of thorns?

'Black hair is best!' says Naomi Sims, famous black American model.

Black hair has been the subject of discussion since the days when it was discovered that some grease, plus some heat (nobody had figured how much of each), would produce the desired amount of straightness and make the wearer 'socially acceptable'. Straight hair was 'good', kinky hair was 'bad'. Many black people still suffer from these very limited descriptions of hair. We have employed all kinds of tactics to straighten our hair, including the axle grease/hot rod treatment! The basic idea was okay, but the methods were decidedly painful, resulting in lots of singed fingers and hair. Other more brave women, hands wrapped in rags, 'pressed' their hair with a flat can. Another adventurous woman discovered that a solution of boiled lye and hot fat would make waves. It also burned the scalp, but nobody seemed to bother about that in the quest for beauty. Black women in America struggled along with these makeshift methods until Madam Walker, a native of Delta, Louisiana in America, adapted an iron comb which could be heated and successfully used to make black hair straight. The Marcel iron invented in 1908 was also employed in flattening black and white people's hair quite successfully. It must have been at this point that the hairdressing business got off its knees and on to its feet. The development of pomades and oils to use in conjunction with these irons followed soon afterwards, and the hairdressing business was born.

The problem, of course, was that some black people left their mother country in such a hurry that it was impossible to pack any combs and ornaments, or even to recall many of the elaborate hair styles worn back in Africa. Styles were certainly never limited to what came to be known as the 'afro'. African women dressed their hair in many styles, even wearing their hair in what are now termed 'European' styles. Brought to a strange

country in unhospitable circumstances, many of these styles were forgotten or lost due to expedience. Everybody worked, and worked hard, and it was impossible to do anything more elaborate than tie a scarf around the head and proceed from there.

After all of these permutations, today's hair care must certainly seem a doddle. The days when the only choice was between hot pressing or the 'natural' look have passed into antiquity. Today the choices are limitless. Black hair isn't necessarily political. We would hazard the guess that black women just want natural-looking, manageable, healthy hair. If that means relaxing, wearing a well-cut 'natural' style, plaits, cornrows or the like, so be it. Black hair can look good all the time and, with some knowledge, and an intelligent use of the many products on the market today, it's not difficult. It's not easy, but it's not impossible either. Take some time to learn about your hair — and about the products available, and don't expect miracles. Learn about its texture, type and how to care for it. Know about its advantages and limitations. Don't just throw up your hands in exasperation; there are products which will tame your hair, and keep it healthy and manageable. There are probably more products for black hair care on the market now than ever before. A word of caution: don't try to use all of them the first week. Select the few that suit your hair and use them unashamedly — and your hair will react. The decision is not between natural or dead straight hair any more; it's now possible to control both texture and curl to get the look you want.

Of course, hair can be difficult — and people too. It's just a matter of learning the best way to handle the situation. Should you relax your hair? Should you wear some variation of the natural? If you do, which style is best and can be most easily altered to break the monotony of wearing the same hair style all the time? No matter which style you decide on, there is one thing that is certain — you must be willing to learn to care for it. Black hair is probably the most versatile in the world! What! You don't believe me? Well, why not? It's possible, once black hair has been relaxed, to do just about anything with it. This gives hairdressers much more scope than they themselves have ever realised.

Despite propaganda to the contrary, black hair *does* grow, at a rate of about half an inch a month. There are conditions, however, which dermatologists refer to as the 'short hair syndrome'. This just means that short hair sometimes runs in families and, in those rare cases, there is not much that can be done to speed up the rate of growth. But don't despair, most hair problems are man-(and woman-) made and not the fault of our ancestors.

Hair doesn't 'grow' or 'not grow'. It's not that simple. Your hair grows in cycles — faster in summer and slower in winter. The cycles last between two and five years. Your hair may be in a 'resting' state when, unluckily, some other tragedy may befall you, like an illness or hair loss from a badly done perm. Even pregnancy can affect your hair. Most hair loss is only temporary, so don't worry too much unless it persists.

What is it?

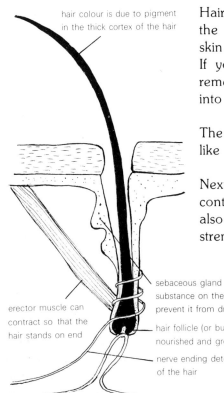

hair colour is due to pigment in the thick cortex of the hair

erector muscle can contract so that the hair stands on end

sebaceous gland pours an oily substance on the hair to prevent it from drying out

hair follicle (or bulb) — the hair is nourished and grows from here

nerve ending detects movement of the hair

blood capillaries

Hair is an extension of the skin, to be sure, and it's affected by the same things that add to or detract from the health of the skin. You can't have healthy hair if the rest of you is unhealthy. If you've been reading magazine articles you will probably remember that your hair is composed of *keratin*, and divided into three layers.

The first layer is called the *cuticle* (outer) and consists of scale-like cells pointing in the direction of the hair ends, ie down.

Next, elongated and fibrous, composed of keratin and containing the colour-giving melanin, is the *cortex*. Here, we also find the fibres that give hair its elasticity and, therefore, its strength.

protective outer layer (or cuticle)

cortex

central core or medulla

A cross-section of one strand of your hair

Last of all is the *medulla*. or inside layer, which consists of round cells and gives the hair its body. What you don't see is the hair root; at the end of this is the hair bulb, and that's where all the action takes place. The bulb is connected to the blood supply and nourished by it.

Why is some hair straight and some hair curly?

Have a look at the pictures here. They should make the reason clear.

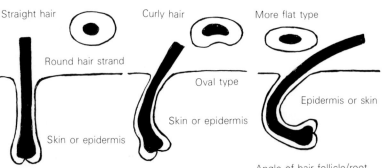

Straight hair

Round hair strand

Skin or epidermis

Note position of follicle

Curly hair

Oval type

Skin or epidermis

Hair root — note angle of follicle/root

More flat type

Epidermis or skin

Angle of hair follicle/root will give kinky or very curly effect to hair.

How can I tell if my hair is healthy?

Examine a few hairs for porosity; that is, how much and how quickly do they absorb water? Have a tug; do they snap back and have they retained their elasticity? Healthy hair can stretch to fifty per cent of its length. Does water bounce off your hair, or does it quickly absorb moisture? If it does, it may be easier to relax, but will eventually become over-processed as it absorbs more and more of the relaxer and is depleted completely of its elasticity. The degree of porosity is regulated by the cuticle (outer layer). An absorbent cuticle resembles a pineapple that's been hacked at. It has a shredded look which indicates thirsty hair. Your task is to soothe and smooth that cuticle so that it closes and seals in its natural moisture.

Fragile

'Black hair is fragile.' How often have we been told this? Many times — I've even said it myself! If you look at the illustration in the box on p 42 you'll see the three types of hair; our hair is the tightly curled one. Because of this particular configuration, it is also weak; every turn of every curl makes it weaker than Caucasian hair. If you have access to a magnifying glass you will be able to see that it is thicker in some parts and thinner in others. This is why, whether relaxed or natural, black hair has to be handled carefully or it will break. Black hair is very easy to stretch, especially when it's wet and therefore at its weakest. Our hair is the way it is because it was designed to protect our skulls from the hot sun of Africa. You will notice that people from colder climates have lighter coloured hair that is fine in texture; this enables *their* skulls to receive the optimum amount of sun! It's just nature's way of looking after her children.

The 'good' hair/'bad' hair syndrome

There's not much more black women can do to their hair, except beat it with a stick! We've tried just about everything else. Over the years, we have laboured under the misconception that there was something 'wrong' with our hair, just because it didn't fall down our backs in undulating waves like Caucasian hair — and that's a fact. It's been constructed to stay put; as such it does its job extremely well. So there's nothing 'wrong' or 'bad' about black hair, there never was. While we try to get our hair straight, white women work just as hard to put some curl into theirs! Their hair may go limp at times, and can be a problem, but they don't call it 'bad'. Oriental hair is very straight and correspondingly difficult to curl or wave. Consider the Chinese or Japanese woman who may want a curly look; it's as difficult for

her to 'bend' her hair as it is for us to straighten ours. These things should never be considered problems, however, just something to be dealt with honestly. It's time we 'came out' from behind closed doors, and stopped hiding all the facts about our hair. Remember, the permanent wave machine was invented because *white* women wanted to change *their* hair. What's more, wouldn't it be awfully boring if we all looked the same?

Why hair loss?

You can well afford to lose one hundred and fifty hairs every day – and not go bald. If you lose more, and all from one place, well, maybe then you have a problem. Are you worried about anything? Are you pregnant? Are you using any drugs? Are you applying too much heat to your hair? All or any one of these things may damage your hair. Unfortunately, it's easier to pinpoint the causes of hair loss than it is to outline the cause of hair growth.

Weathervane

Everything, but everything affects your hair; deficiencies you may not be aware of; disease; even extreme weight loss. Hair, like skin, is a reflection of your general health. So, if your hair is coming out, check your life-style and your diet. Desperate? Try taking kelp (seaweed) three times a day; it's a source of sulphur and helps the hair to grow.

Wearing your hair too tightly cornrowed or plaited can cause it to break off because it doesn't allow the scalp to move. So, if you've elected to plait because you've had problems with relaxing, don't ruin it by leaving the plaits in too long. If your hair is relaxed and you want to keep your style, learn to roll it up in a proper pin curl, and *DO* use end papers.

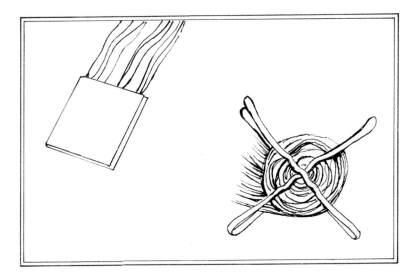

What's your type?

Hair comes in many shapes and forms, but right now it's texture we're interested in. Hair may be normal, dry or oily; coarse, fine or medium in texture; or it may be a combination of these. Hair may be described as 'fine', but not 'thin', for the word 'fine' refers to its texture, and not its density, ie the number of hairs per square inch. It's possible to have fine hair that is thick, and coarse hair that is not very abundant. Baby fine hair, because it is actually very small in diameter, often looks shorter than it actually is; coarse hair will look thicker. Along with the psychological implications, the 'natural' look, practically speaking, was probably the best thing to come along in years. Like plaits, it gives the hair and scalp a chance to rest. Black women sometimes believe their hair doesn't grow as fast as Caucasian hair but, as we have said, this is not necessarily true. It's usually treatment and breakage that cause hair damage and loss.

If your hair *is* thin and lacks body, it needs tender, loving care. Make good and frequent use of body-building shampoos. Shampoos containing balsam will make your hair too soft. Avoid harsh relaxers, and always use shampoos and conditioners; they coat the hair shaft and give a more full look; let hair dry naturally. Whatever you do, do it gently.

Baby fine hair has a reputation for being thin, wispy and hard to handle. This is possibly true, but personal experience with our own less than wispy growth proves that fine hair can be almost indestructible! Baby fine hair usually does need a lot of help to make it look full and attractive. It can appear limp and lose its curl in a tick. A good cut can prevent its fly-away look, and a colour rinse often gives the illusion of more hair.

Relaxed hair that is fine sometimes has a tendency to lose its body and look lank. If this happens you might try to find out more about a new method that has been developed in the USA. This involves applying a body perm, a method which was formerly only available to remedy the fine hair problems of white clients.

Your hair and scalp need gentle stimulation every day. Why not give yourself a massage while watching the television or the latest video – or even just sitting? Just spread your fingers apart and slowly rotate the scalp with the pads of your fingers for about five minutes. This promotes circulation, bringing nourishment to the scalp and hair, and helps distribute the natural oils which make your hair look and feel healthy.

Split ends are easy to see; your hair looks like a shredded rope with the resultant 'my hair doesn't grow' syndrome. They are caused by over-processing, too frequent blow drying and the use of alkaline shampoos. It *does* grow, but when dry ends split they have to be cut off. It's the only remedy. If the ends aren't trimmed, the split will simply travel up the hair shaft and the remedy will be even more drastic. If you want to apply one of the 'repair' products on the market, you'll have to be quick and diligent. It's still best to trim the ends, and make sure you avoid the condition in the future.

Brushes and brushing

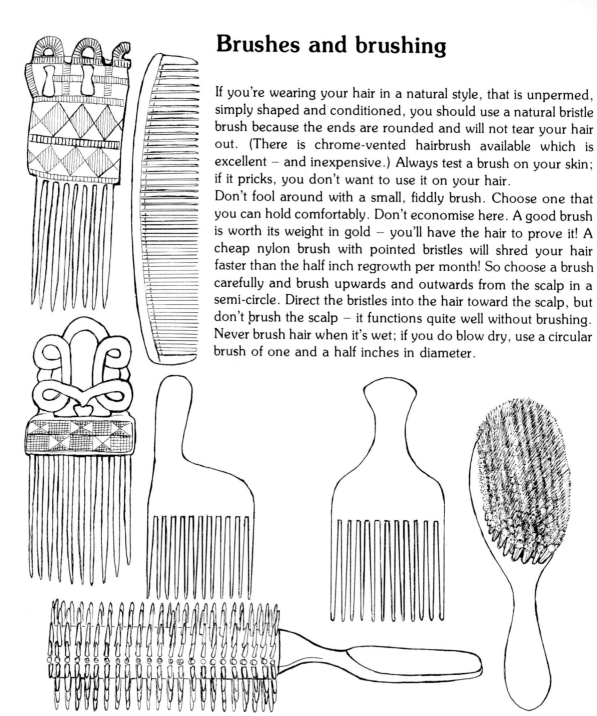

If you're wearing your hair in a natural style, that is unpermed, simply shaped and conditioned, you should use a natural bristle brush because the ends are rounded and will not tear your hair out. (There is chrome-vented hairbrush available which is excellent – and inexpensive.) Always test a brush on your skin; if it pricks, you don't want to use it on your hair.

Don't fool around with a small, fiddly brush. Choose one that you can hold comfortably. Don't economise here. A good brush is worth its weight in gold – you'll have the hair to prove it! A cheap nylon brush with pointed bristles will shred your hair faster than the half inch regrowth per month! So choose a brush carefully and brush upwards and outwards from the scalp in a semi-circle. Direct the bristles into the hair toward the scalp, but don't brush the scalp – it functions quite well without brushing. Never brush hair when it's wet; if you do blow dry, use a circular brush of one and a half inches in diameter.

Treat yourself to two brushes and a wide toothed comb. Keep them clean (wash them in a solution of warm water, detergent and some Dettol), and don't ever use anybody else's comb or brush. You're not Desdemona, so forget about the one hundred strokes; a few well-placed strokes which carry the oils down to the ends of your hair are sufficient.

Coarse, thick hair

You're probably lucky. Your hair will always look nice and hold a set. It may be a bit hard to handle, as the hair strands are larger than the wispy baby fine ones. What you want first is a good hair cut. You can do just about anything with your hair, relax, blow dry, the lot. Your hair may be spiky if it's very coarse, especially if you come from West Africa, and tight curls may be a problem. Have you noticed that tight curls become even tighter when it's hot and humid and when it rains? Of course, massage gently – but then, you knew I was going to say that. Brush often, a bit harder perhaps, but don't over-do it. Use a shampoo that contains lanolin or balsam to make the hair softer and easier to handle. Follow with a cream rinse.

Problems

If you've never straightened or used tints on your hair, this section isn't for you. However, if you have done any tinting, rinsing or dyeing – read on. You might find that as a result of doing various things to your hair it has become dry and brittle and difficult to manage. There's really no getting around it – if you want to have healthy, lively hair, no matter how you wear it, you have to be good to it. Don't starve it! Hair is for the most part protein, which must be replenished. Dyeing, straightening and tinting rob the hair of its natural oils. If you're not careful, one day you might wake up and find your hair is split, broken, and terrible! What should you do?

Split ends and dryness are the most frequent results of straightened or dyed hair. They can also be the result of too much time spent in the sun or on the beach without a scarf or hat. Avoid using too much heat, whether in the form of heated combs or excessive blow drying. Use conditioners made of hydrolised animal protein (read the labels), these are absorbed *into* the hair shaft. Don't ever brush your hair (or allow it to be brushed) while it's still warm: the cuticles will still be open.
Always use end papers when setting your hair. If you do use a hairspray, be sure that it's an anti-humidity one.

There are products on the market to please everybody and to remedy just about *every* kind of hair problem: conditioning creams and lotions, thick and thin, store bought, and home-made. Whichever one you try, use it regularly. Don't abandon it if the results aren't instantaneous – give it at least three months to work.

If you have tired hair, try one of the following:

Hot oil treatment

First shampoo your hair and towel it dry. Then, with a piece of cotton wool, apply warmed olive or baby oil to the entire scalp. Moisten fingertips with oil and apply to ends of hair. Wring out a towel in very hot water and wrap it around your head. Leave the towel on until it cools. Alternatively, apply a deep penetrating conditioner and sit under a dryer set to *LOW* for twenty minutes.

Dry and damaged?

Remedy as for split ends – you'll need a good trim. Damaged hair has to be repaired by 'rebuilding' it by the use of polymers which literally mend the hair.

Dry hair

Your hair may feel like dry bramble; be spiky and difficult to manage; look dull. If this is the case . . .

Your under-active sebaceous glands may not be to blame; look to your shampoo, the weather, your central heating, too much hot pressing and/or blow dying. Any or all of these things may be the root cause of dry hair. Treat it with a mild conditioning shampoo every five to seven days. Use an instant conditioner every time and rub a light conditioning cream on your scalp and the ends of your hair. Brush gently. Do use a deep conditioning treatment once a month.

The Treatment

Heat some olive (safflower) or almond oil in a cup by placing it in a saucepan of hot water. Section off your hair, saturate a wad of cotton wool with oil and apply to the sectioned hair. Wring out a towel in hot water and wrap it around your head until it cools. Repeat this three times.

OR

Apply oil to your hair and scalp and cover with a shower cap. For a secure fit, cover the lot with a scarf and let your hair 'steam' for twenty minutes.

Be sure to shampoo until all traces of oil have been removed. A vinegar rinse may help you here. One of the many deep conditioning treatments on the market can also be used instead of the olive oil.

Oily hair

The oils that produce a shiny skin seem to be less of a problem with black people who seldom have oily scalps. If your hair appears oily, it may be caused by the application of too heavy oils or pomades, rather than over-active glands, which attract dirt and dust and prevent the scalp from breathing. If your hair is really oily (rather than greasy), curtail your intake of greasy food and think: are you having romantic problems or taking medication? Anything like that may upset your metabolism and cause an oily scalp.

The treatment

Your weekly shampoo should be antiseptic and acid-balanced, but don't go overboard and dry out the hair. Alternate with a mild shampoo and a lemon rinse. Let your hair dry naturally. Always use a light hairdressing and avoid too much brushing or massaging, as this will only stimulate those oil glands you want to rest.

Natural hair

(Hair that has not been permed, relaxed or tinted.) Natural hair has a tendency to become dry because the curly structure prevents the hair's natural oils from travelling down the hair shaft to the ends. If you want to keep your natural hair looking that way you should shampoo and condition it weekly. There are a number of shampoos on the market formulated especially for your hair, but look for non-alkaline or oil-based shampoos. We're not heavy on a lot of brushing, but we do recommend a few well-chosen strokes with a good bristle brush. Remember how delicate your hair is when wet, so *don't pull*. Dry naturally, whenever you can. Comb it with a wide-toothed comb.

Balsam, while not advisable for permed hair, is excellent for your natural hair; it will make it soft and easier to comb. Natural hair should be trimmed and shaped every few weeks to suit *your* face – try a barber!

Normal hair

Normal hair, like normal skin, is well-balanced, neither oily nor dry, and has a healthy and attractive appearance. Don't worry if it's not shiny. Black hair, because of its corkscrew shape, is not naturally shiny.

Shampoo regularly with a mild shampoo and condition with an instant conditioner. If you relax your hair, then follow directions for relaxed hair.

Salon relaxing

– it'll never be the same . . .

Relaxed/permed hair has been changed forever, or at least for the life of that particular head of hair. The solution, containing about 2.5 per cent sodium hydroxide (lye), changes the molecular structure of the hair. It actually rearranges the keratin chains, leaving the hair straight, or less curly. How? It works by softening the outer (cuticle) layer of the hair shaft, and allowing the relaxer to enter the inner (cortex) layer. A neutraliser is then applied to stop the process, and zap, your once curly hair is now straight or as straight as you want it to be. More than eight minutes of this treatment and your hair will dissolve!

Plaits or cornrowing notwithstanding, relaxed hair is easier to manage. It's certainly easier to comb and condition, but you never get something for nothing. Relaxed hair, like any hair, has to be cared for. Relaxing removes some of the hair's natural moisture, and that has to be replaced after *every* shampoo; no backsliding allowed. Follow some simple directions.

Never delay having a retouch because the permed ends will now be stronger than the roots, and you can pull your hair out when you comb it. Always use a conditioner after every shampoo, a non-alkaline one, of course. Balsam makes permed hair too soft, so avoid it. Keep your ends well-conditioned and trimmed. Where there are *DOS*, there are always *DON'TS*. Get to know your hairdresser; don't go to a stranger whose work you don't know. Try to see some of his/her work first. Don't book your first appointment when the shop is likely to be crowded. Give the operator time to examine your hair. Tell her (or him) if you've been taking any medication; it may affect the outcome. Never consider having a perm if you already have a relaxer in your hair, or if your hair is dry and damaged. Relaxing certainly won't improve the look of it, and you'll end up with limp, lacklustre hair that is over-processed; hair which may have to be cut off!! How many times can we repeat this rule!

Never, never put one relaxer on top of another, unless you like the look of *BALD*.

Curly perm

Your curly perm will always look attractive if you remember to shampoo regularly, once or twice a week, and apply your curl activator to wet hair each morning. It should contain water, but needn't be too greasy or heavy. Conditioning after a shampoo will keep your curl pattern intact, and a trim and shaping will improve the look.

If you've been using henna or any metallic dyes, allow your hair to grow out before using a relaxer. Out also are too hot combs, too hot dryers and using a relaxer if your scalp is sore or broken out. In other words, don't relax unless you – and therefore your hair – are in tip top condition.

Your curly perm will have been accomplished by applying a solution of ammonium thioglycolate to the hair. It immediately enters the cortex, where it breaks down the sulphur and hydrogen S bonds, producing as much (or as little) curl as you want. 'Thio' is much more gentle to our curly bits, but it can only be used on virgin hair. Once the hair has been softened, a neutraliser is applied to halt the process. If the process is not carried out properly, you'll end up with non-existent cuticle inbrications (hair that looks like fish scales all standing up!). It's not a pretty sight and not a pretty feeling. Your hair will have the appearance of a limp squid.

The curly perm is very popular with black women. It came along just when the charm of the natural was on the wane and women wanted something new and different. There are many, we repeat many ways to wear this new look. It can be cut and shaped, swept back or up – as you please. With some imagination and a bit of patience, you can make your curly perm individually *YOU*. We will have more to say about 'thio' perms later.

You've probably heard the expression 'keep your hair on'. Well, if you're serious about it, you'd be wise always to request a *strand test* before your hair is relaxed. You should do this every time, because your body chemistry may have altered. Have your stylist snip off a bit of your hair and test it for elasticity, and to ascertain the time needed to relax in the solution he is using. Don't be afraid to ask questions of your hairdresser, the more knowledgeable you are about your hair, the easier his or her job will be.

Fancy a new look for your curly perm? After shampooing your hair, apply a deep conditioning hot oil treatment. Rinse out and blot your hair dry, then apply a small amount of cream hairdressing and tong your hair into a new style.

What a change!

Relaxing your hair at home

The art of hairdressing is best learned in due course – at best it's not a do-it-yourself occupation, and should be left to professionals. Relaxing your hair at home is like having a baby at home; it can go very well but, just in case it doesn't, it's good to have a professional around to tell you what to do.

If you've been neglecting your hair, under no circumstances should you consider adding insult to injury by applying a relaxer. (And that includes a curly perm!) If you've been colouring your hair or wearing wigs or tight cornrows, give your hair a chance to rest. You'll get better results.

Women will have a go at relaxing their hair at home for many reasons, time and money being two of them. Often, having damaged or over-processed hair is enough to keep a woman from returning to a salon. Some women are very good with their hair and can be successful working with a 'home permanent kit'. Again, the same rules apply as for a salon perm. It might be wise to have a professional perm, and then do the re-touch yourself.

There are many home permanent kits available. Remember, however, the warning on the back of these kits says '*for professional use only*'; that lets the manufacturer off the hook in the event of you burning your hair or having any other problems that might have to be remedied in a salon.

What you'll need

Mirror
Good lighting
Plastic gloves
Timer
Tinting brush
Wide-toothed comb
Towel for shoulders

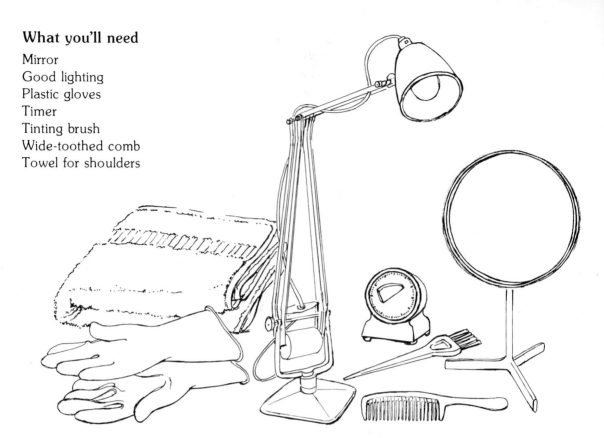

Some dos

- Assemble everything you need.
- Do a patch test *AND* a strand test.
- Read the directions very carefully.
- Apply vaseline to hairline, ears and neck – don't be stingy!
- Use a good mirror and a light bright enough to see properly.
- Enlist the aid of a friend or relative, to help with the back.
- Use a timer.
- Stop immediately if the relaxer begins to burn; rinse out with the shampoo provided.
- Use a tint brush to apply relaxer – lay it on with the brush, never rub it in and only work on untreated hair.
- Use a towel to cover your shoulders.

And don'ts

- Never relax hair that is dry, brittle or damaged.
- Never leave lotion on more than eight minutes.
- Never use brush rollers to set the hair.
- Never use one relaxer on top of another.
- Never use a relaxer if your scalp is broken.
- Never forget to use end papers when setting hair.
- Never use a *HOT* setting to dry your hair.
- Never use over henna.
  If your hair is already permed, and you'd like a 'curly perm' look, set on small rods – it works!

Ready, set . . .

Just before you're ready to set your hair, spray it with a bit of neat cream rinse; it will make your hair easier to handle. Follow this with a light spray with a solution of vinegar and water. Why? Well, it completes the job of restoring your pH level. Wait a few minutes between these last two processes.

Get under your dryer and relax. Once your hair is dry, and you've removed the rollers, rub a small amount of light hair oil on the palms of your hands and apply it to your hair. You're now ready for the comb-out.

How to go straight – two easy ways

The mature women (or her daughter) may not want the curly perm or plaits, and for her there is an alternative.

Defrissage (*day-free-saje*): It's so old, that it's new!

The process of 'frying' hair has been revolutionised, thanks to Madam Walker's iron comb; today you can use a thermal comb – which is even better.

Hot combing is not new, and just when we think it's died a death, it comes back stronger than ever. Temporary though it may be, it can be the answer, the alternative to over-processed, chemically relaxed hair. Hot combing is much easier than it used to be, and if you use Lustrasilk or one of the lotion relaxers, like Vigorol, not only can this process be simple, the result can be as satisfactory as a chemical relaxer. (Vigorol is a 'thio' process and permanent; Lustrasilk is temporary.)

These 'relaxers' work by softening the hair bonds and building in moisture, so that the hair can be hot combed without excessive use of grease. In this way you can achieve a lighter, more professional look.

Any woman who has suffered from damaged hair would do well to investigate one of the non-lye based relaxers that are fast becoming the trend; they're easier to use and, providing you follow the directions very carefully, you should have excellent results.

The limitation to these new methods is, as in the case of hot combing, that it only lasts from shampoo to shampoo. The 'thio' perm is longer lasting, and can be applied every four weeks. The advantage is that both these methods will allow your poor, tired, demoisturised hair to rest, while looking nice and being manageable at the same time.

Lustrasilk doesn't work on the 'thio' principle, but makes use of a porosity solution to build in moisture. This means that a warm comb can be used without adding any grease or oil. The result is a finished look, free of grease. It really does work wonderfully. Shampoo with a good shampoo and *follow the directions.* Choice? you've got it! Wear it permed, natural, cornrowed, plaited, curly – or take the curl out with one of the new 'thio' perms.

Hot combing

What you'll need:
Protein conditioner
Scalp cream
Thermal comb (used carefully)
Wide-toothed comb
Blow dryer (used on *LOW* setting)
Tissues

- Shampoo and towel dry hair. Apply pressing cream lightly to scalp.
- Section hair into four to six parts and pin.
- Press each section separately and pin.
- If you're not using a thermal comb, be sure that you 'tissue test' your comb for scorching. If it burns the tissues, it's too hot for your hair. Mind your ears.
- When you've finished pressing, either roll, pin or tong your hair.

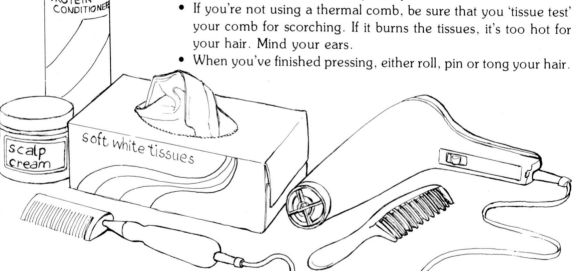

The 'thio perm'

(the 'wave' of the future)

In addition to the variety of cream relaxers already on the market, another kind of straightener/relaxer is now available – the liquid relaxer or 'thio' perm. Shake hands with 'thio'; it won't work miracles, but it can remove a lot of the hassle of achieving neat, easy to manage hair.

The major difference between the 'thio' perm and the others is that 'thio' softens the S bonds (lye based relaxers dissolve them completely) so that they can be rearranged into a straight pattern. The sodium chloride perm works faster, to be sure, whereas the 'thio' solution can be left on the hair for up to twenty minutes.

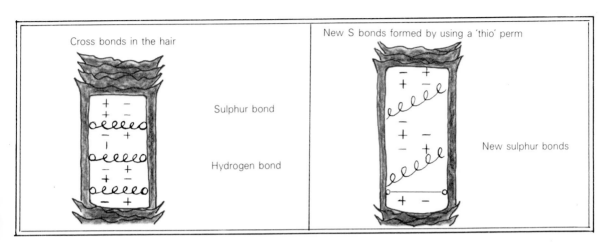

Cross bonds in the hair

New S bonds formed by using a 'thio' perm

Sulphur bond

Hydrogen bond

New sulphur bonds

How does it work? Easy. The 'thio' in your perm is ammonium thioglycolate, the same ingredient that your curly perm is made of. It contains two active ingredients; ammonia and thioglycolic acid (not as caustic as sodium hydroxide, the active ingredient in most chemical relaxers). Remember that the S bonds of your hair must be altered to show any visible difference in the curl pattern. The 'thio' perm is a one-step process. Once the liquid has been applied and the ammonia has penetrated the hair, the thioglycolic acid softens the S bonds; the hair is then smoothed with the back of a comb, or with the fingers, resulting in an alteration in the curl pattern of black hair, changing the tight curl to a more manageable wave. It's as simple as that. Not straight enough? Well then, you can apply cream and press with a warm iron. Unlike Lustrasilk, the 'thio' perm retains its loose curl pattern through shampoos until a retouch is needed.

As we used to say in the old days, 'My hair's not kinky, the waves are just close together'. Well, this new perm will make sure the waves are *not* too close together.

A cautious note at this point. Be sure to follow instructions carefully; this applies to all relaxers. You can use both Lustrasilk and Vigorol at home quite safely. Be sure that your hair is in good condition, neither dry nor brittle. Be sure that your scalp is not scratched and if you've been colouring your hair, do a strand test to determine its condition. Last, but not least, before going ahead, be sure that you have read and clearly understood the directions for use of your new 'wave'.

Styling

Styling shouldn't be the problem it sometimes is. Whatever your hairstyle, it should begin with a good cut, one that suits your face (not your friend's or the model's on the magazine cover). Examine yourself carefully and critically; then decide just who you are and what you want to look like. Once you've got over that hurdle you should be able to face your shortcomings. If you have a short neck, you want a hairstyle that doesn't emphasise it, no matter how 'fashionable'. Having long hair is lovely, but it shouldn't be trained to resemble a floor mop. All hair styles benefit from a bit of trimming and a bit of shaping. Hair that looks as if you're going to a cocktail party at nine am is out of place, no matter how glamorous the style.

Your hair should always look nice, not only when it's freshly done. It will look good if you select a style that flatters your particular texture of hair. Some styles work better on coarse, thick hair than on fine hair. Don't get hung up on face shapes; remember that you have to consider your own overall shape and height. For example, if your hair is very short and your face is round, and you're a big girl, you will want a soft style that will help to soften your outline, rather than one which is close to your head. Proportion is what you should aim for.

Find a style that you can manage yourself without rushing off to the hairdresser at the drop of a hat. A curly perm pushed back and held in place with a decorative comb, or smoothed with setting gel, or a well-placed braid will work wonders when you've been asked out and haven't time to make elaborate preparations.

Remember, the style is in the cut, so pay attention when your hair is being cut or trimmed – you'll have to live with the results. Learn to roll, pin curl and restyle your own hair and train it to keep a set between appointments. Use end papers, and remember to keep all rollers, pins and combs used very clean. You can set your hair very well with toilet paper, tissues or brown paper.

Stay away from woolly hats – they're especially bad for hair around the hairline.

Combless hairstyling

In the last ten years the comb has taken somewhat of a back seat in favour of the combless hairstyle. With the growing popularity of plaits, cornrowing, wrapping, twisting, etc there are countless artistic ways which are open to the black woman if she wishes to vary her hairstyle, perhaps between perms or just for the novelty of change itself.

The advantage is that these 'combless' styles stay put for weeks and, if cared for, will continue to look attractive. Admittedly, they involve several hours of sitting. In Africa hair dressing is a social occasion where a woman has her hair done over a day, during which time she visits, gossips, takes care of her children, cooks, then returns to have her hair style completed. The recent combination of the ingenuity of both hairdresser and customer has meant many new styles that work very well and are fascinating to see.

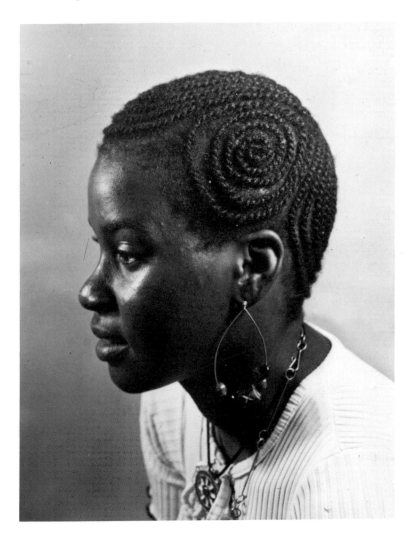

Cornrows

These are never in or out of style, but always there. Every black woman has had her hair cornrowed or plaited at some time during her childhood. Now, suddenly, grown-up ladies are also styling their hair this way. Your cornrows will stay in and stay neat if you follow some easy directions.

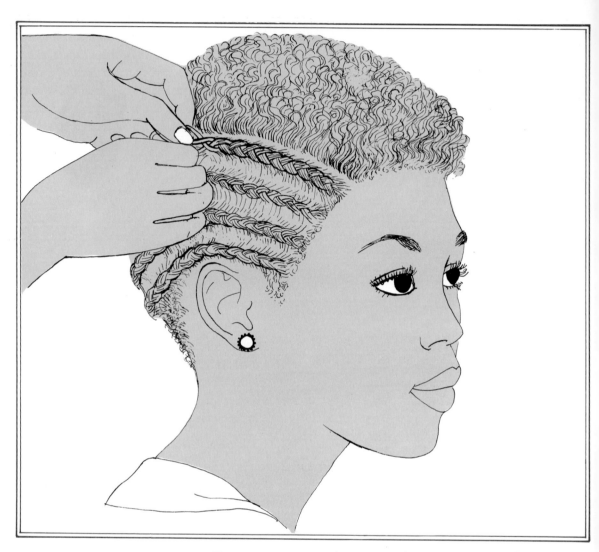

Shampoo every eight to ten days; cover your hair with a stocking cap. Condition it in the same way. Rinse well and avoid pulling. The ends may need clipping. Remember that the idea is to rest your hair and allow it to grow, so don't braid it too tightly; this will only add pressure to the scalp. Wear a scarf to bed.

If cornrows or plaits remain in the hair too long or are woven too tightly, you'll succeed only in pulling your hair out! Massage your scalp and be sure to use a light spray-on conditioner regularly.

Of course you can do your own extensions if you have the patience. You can cornrow your hair in front and leave the back loose. It's your style to vary as you please.

Here's how to do it. Using real or artificial hair, take a few strands and begin a quarter of an inch before the end of your own hair. Combine 'fake' hair with your own and simply plait in slowly.

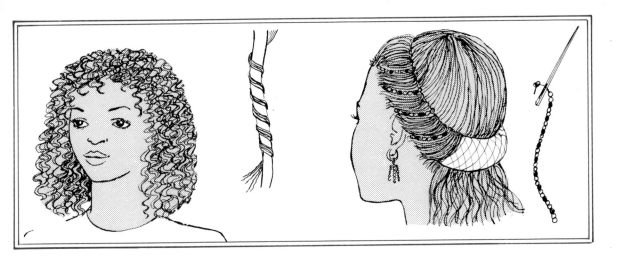

Wrapping

This is another choice for women who refuse to relax their hair chemically. Wrapping is similar to cornrowing, but the look is somewhat bulkier, in a controlled way. It will look as though you have more hair than you have. Lift a section of your hair and 'weave' it into a straight line, either vertically or horizontally. Secure the end hairs with a hairgrip until you are completely finished; then weave all the ends together. If you remember how you accomplished the 'add-on' extensions, then you'll have found the knack of wrapping.

Wrap and twist

This may be the answer if you have long, thick, natural hair. It's a neat and very easy style, and you can make it plain or fancy. Buy a 'filler' (these used to be called 'rats' in the old days), pin it to your head and roll your own hair around it. If you're going out, dress it with fancy beads, pins or combs.

Hairweaving

Some of us do not look good in plaits, and others of us do not want a curly perm, so what's left? You might ask. The answer may be to have a hairweave. Hairweaving has been in the market place for nearly as long as hot combing, but it's never been as popular. It's much too time-consuming and too expensive.

There are several methods of weaving, some of which require less than the three to four and a half hours usually required. Real or synthetic hair is literally woven into the customer's own hair, so close to the scalp that it is virtually impossible to detect. This is similar to the method in which extensions are added in cornrowing. Literally sewing hanks of hair on to the customer's own hair is another method.

Very short hair can be improved by this method and medium length hair will assume a more full look. This could be the answer for women who wear wigs most of the time (not something we would recommend). Hairweaving, provided it is not too tight, gives the scalp and hair a chance to rest, nourish itself and grow.

The art of the shampoo

Hair is an extension of skin, and many of the same rules for tender, loving care apply. Beginning at square one, we cleanse (shampoo), tone (massage), and moisturise (condition), both our hair and our skin. The idea is to remove the ravages of pollution and cosmetics, and to condition it to retain the look of healthy hair. Too often these basics are obscured in the rush to do too many things at the same time. There are shampoos that promise to do everything but start up your car. Be wary! If a shampoo promises too many things, rest assured it won't accomplish any of them very well; you'll end up with hair that is neither clean nor healthy and be in time for the 'dry, brittle' queue. Save yourself the marathon sprint with soapy hair by gathering all the things you need first.

- Shampoo for 'oily' hair, 'dry' hair, 'damaged' or 'permed' hair.
- Towels
- Dryer – if you plan to use one – set on *WARM* or *LOW*, of course.

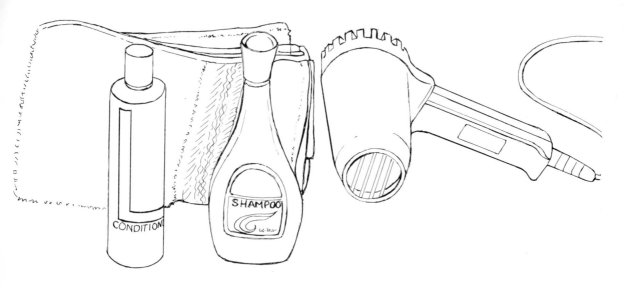

- Ready? Massage scalp just a little to loosen dirt and to encourage it to move.
- Wet hair completely with warm water.
- Pour a small amount of shampoo into the palm of your hands and gently massage it into your hair, working it well in. Do this twice and rinse until the water is clear and your hair feels clean.
- Towel dry and apply your conditioner.
- Rinse again – don't leave a trace of anything unless it's supposed to remain on your hair. The last rinse should be with cool water to seal the hair cuticle so that the conditioner can do its job.

Be sure to allow yourself enough time for this, because it shouldn't be a rushed job. The best way to dry your hair is naturally, by blotting it with a towel. But we know you'll use some kind of dryer most of the time. So, never use a 'hot' setting, you'll just undo all the work of the conditioner, by burning your hair dry. We *know* it's faster, but it's *not* better unless you want the hair on your head to resemble a scouring pad! Remember, your natural oils aren't pumped up with the ferocity of a petrol pump; they have to have time to replace themselves. If you keep depleting them, your hair will suffer. Blow drying more than once a week is asking for trouble.

The wonderful world of conditioners, moisturisers, rinses and the miracles they perform – with your help

First of all, let me just say that if I could hereby conjure up some magic formula or solution which would make your hair sprout like spring grass – I'd be rich! There is no easy solution but, with some patience and time, it is not as difficult as you may think to get, and keep, your hair beautiful. Know what you're using, always.

You've shampooed (see page 64) and dried your hair, now what next?

Rinses

Their job is to seal the hair shaft, detangle the hair making it easier to comb, and then remove the remainder of any soap left. They work much the same as a cleanser works on your face. There are three types of rinse.

Instant

Apply the rinse to your hair according to the instructions. Make sure you only leave it on for the time stated. Rinse off thoroughly.

Deep

These are left on the hair for twenty minutes to an hour, and are often used in conjunction with some kind of heat for better penetration.

Non-rinsable conditioners

These are left on the hair to work until your next shampoo.

Protein and coating conditioners

These feed the hair by filling in broken or split ends. As the hair is composed mainly of protein, these conditioners are especially useful if your hair is permed, tinted or very dry.

Oil conditioners

These are a great help in repairing 'winter hair' that has been ravaged by cold weather and central heating, or hair that has suffered from too much sun. An oil conditioner can come to the rescue when your own natural oils are below par. They're not suitable for fine hair.

Fine hair repair, spray with a light conditioner, and sit under a dryer for thirteen minutes.

Rinses and conditioners have some of the same properties, inasmuch as they make the hair easier to handle by coating the hair shaft, leaving the hair soft, flexible and shiny. Because of their temporary effect, they must be used often, every time you shampoo in fact. Conditioners are to the hair what moisturisers are to the skin. They help protect the hair from the abuses of chemical straighteners, poor diet and pollution.

There are cream rinses that stay on the hair, and cream rinses that are rinsed off; conditioners (usually gelatin based) that coat, fill in and thicken broken or brittle hair. If your conditioner is built into a hairdressing, then it probably is petroleum, mineral or lanolin based. Easy-comb conditioners do just what they say – they make the hair easier to comb because of a combination of softeners and oil.

You need to condition after *every* shampoo. Sorry about that!

Wigs

'Wigs are essential to every person's head as lace is to their clothes . . .'
(*17th century London Chronicle*)
As we know, the ancient Egyptians wore wigs and affected elaborate hairstyles which were not supposed to resemble real hair. Very often wigs denoted rank. The first wigs were made of real hair; later wool and palm leaf fibres were used. Black was the first choice so far as colour was concerned but, later, they grew much more adventurous and mixed henna and indigo to get blues, greens and other colours.

Wigs and hairpieces

Many of us at some time in our lives have been thankful for wigs! Whether they are long, short, afro, curly or straight, they're a great help to a busy woman, and are especially handy for those times when we are unable to pay enough attention to our own hair, are feeling terrible or have been caught in bad weather without an umbrella — and for those times when we just want to look different. Learning a bit about wigs and hairpieces will make them easier to deal with quickly and efficiently. And that's really the point, isn't it? It will take some time to become knowledgeable in 'wiggery', but it's worth it.

We've come a long way from the time when cavemen wore wigs made of goatskin. Ancient Egyptian ladies also wore wigs which were quite elaborate and in different colours. We know that Cleopatra had a selection of wigs as elaborate as those of Elizabeth I.

Your wig may be real, meaning that it's made of either European hair (soft, but expensive), or Oriental hair (coarser than European hair, but half the price). Oriental hair is best in dark shades, because it has to be bleached before dyeing and the dark shades look more natural. Your wig may alternatively be made from one of the new synthetics on the market.

Real hair wigs need almost as much care and attention as your own hair, because they are subject to the same ills, breaking and split ends. They have to be trimmed, washed regularly and conditioned. Today the fakes are so fabulous that they look more like real hair — than real hair! Check the label, because 'real hair'

may mean animal and not *human* hair. Yak hair is used in stage hair and is not suitable for street wear – also, it itches!!!

Frankly fake

The 'miracle' fibres used in most inexpensive wigs today have many advantages, besides the price. Think back to the time you first saw Dynel wigs – they screamed, 'I'm fake and not a very good one at that!' Some of them resembled a recent escapee from a Tarzan film. Well, that's all changed drastically. Synthetic wigs are machine-made; the hairs are stitched on in groups as opposed to being hand sewn (as in real wigs). A small amount of hand sewing is involved in the finish. The use of a stretch or open cap base provides a better fit, and eliminates the need to be fitted. The style has already been baked in, so it never has to be set. Did I hear you say 'great'? Well that's not all. You don't need a wig box or wig block because, unless you really neglect your 'fake', it will retain its shape, even in your handbag.

How to take care of your wig

First of all the motto is 'trim and thin'. Most fakes are, as we said, machine stitched, and that means they have plenty of hair in them. No two heads measure exactly the same, and you have to look at yourself in a good mirror and decide where to trim so that the wig suits your face (and not the wig block in the shop). Wigs should also be thinned a little, as they are usually a bit bushy.

Tender loving care

Your fake will need laundering – how often depends on how much you wear it. Wash it in baby shampoo for best results. Just swish it around in a bowl of warm water and drape it over the taps in the bath tub to dry. Every six to eight weeks is usually sufficient to keep it clean.

Use heated rollers or warm curling tongs *only* if instructed.

Some don'ts

- Don't brush your fake when it's wet. Wait until it is completely dry.
- Don't neglect your own hair when wearing wigs or add-ons.
- Don't wear a wig every day; it's not healthy for your own hair and scalp.
- Don't store your new 'hair' in a plastic bag. Use an old scarf instead.

Do

- Buy wigs made for black women.

Last but not least

If someone compliments you on how *nice* your '*wig*' looks – throw it away because you're wearing it all wrong! A wig should never look like a wig unless you're in the theatre and it's part of a costume.

Your wig should always be trimmed to suit *your* face. If you can't do it, then have it done by a good hairdresser. If it's too shiny, brush some talcum powder through it. That will take the sheen away and make it look more natural.

No loose ends (hairpieces)

If you find a full hair wig uncomfortable, you might like a hairpiece that you can attach to your own hair. It's especially nice for a party. Here's how to 'fix' the thing to your head so that it won't fall into the punch bowl. Make a big pin curl at the back of your head (or wherever you want the hairpiece). Place two hair grips across one another to form an 'X'. Place hairpiece over the 'X' and use a few more grips to secure it. The hairpiece should then be perfectly safe and should not shift. Lastly comb some of your own hair over the join. If your hair is very fine or very short, buy a 'grip tooth' comb and sew it to the hairpiece with nylon thread.

What can you do with hairpieces?

Just about anything you'd like to do! No matter what kind of weather you're faced with, hot or cold, wet or dry, your hairpiece will allow you to look well groomed no matter what the occasion. The choice is strictly yours. You can choose from full wigs, switches/falls, pin-on hair or a cascade of curls. Of course we all have the odd emergency; no salon appointment, no electric curlers, just panic and an important appointment – well then it's all right to pop on your favourite hairpiece, but never, please, never use a wig to disguise a dirty head – a wig or add-on should be used to mirror another you; it's not a disguise. You can achieve a straight look one day and a curly one the next, so be clever; practise in front of a mirror, and decide – who am I today?

Falls

Your fall just may be one of the best things that's happened to you in a long time – a chance for the more glamorous you to shine through. Falls come in lengths from ten to twenty-eight inches and are usually (but not always) attached to a comb. Brush your own hair back and gather it into a pony tail (even a short one). Pin with crossed grips which form an 'X', slip the comb over this X, slip in a few hair grips to secure further, and you're on your own. You can dress it up with a braid wound round, or a ribbon or folded scarf if you think the join may be detected.

Falls come in textures that more closely resemble our own hair, so don't be afraid that anyone will detect your secret. For a super-sophisticated look, you could even wind it into a bun high on your head and dress it with combs and/or 'pearls' or a pretty earring.

Gather hair at the nape of the neck and secure with a jewelled pony tail holder, allow remaining hair to fall free.

Wrap a folded scarf around your head and secure it. Wrap your hair around the scarf, allowing some of the scarf to be seen — very colourful.

If your hair is medium length, that is at least ear length, and you're still feeling in a festive mood, part it from ear to ear, comb forward and smooth remaining hair into a pony tail very high on the crown of your head. Attach your fall with 'X' hair grips, comb 'hair' into a 'bun' and secure with long hair pins.

Brush hair smoothly back, so that join is disguised, then, with a brush, pull some hair forward on hairline to soften the look.

When your friends admire your style and ask where you got 'all that hair' — tell them the truth: say, 'I bought it.'

Switches and curls

Change your looks with precision-like speed. Change your image to Diana Ross, Boney M or just a more glamorous you. Gather your hair high over one ear and secure it with an elastic band. Attach a long thick braid, or a hank of hair and let it hang free. Use a sequinned ribbon (for evenings), a velvet band or a thong to hide the join. If you're feeling particular festive, thread silver or gold lace through the braid.

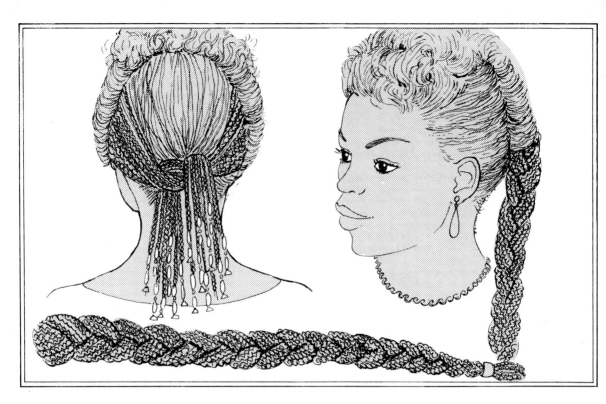

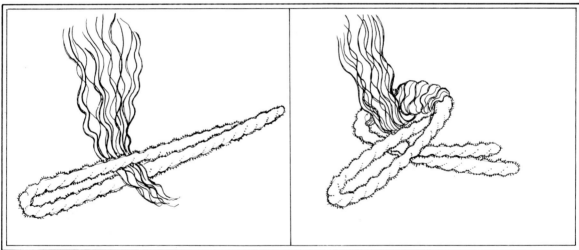

Wearing a kaftan or long dress? Pull your hair back flat, using five to six thin braids (or a switch braided into five or six parts); attach it at the crown. Thread a pipe cleaner into each braid and shape or coil it around your head. Complete the effect with studs or other hair ornaments.

If you are using a demi-wig of soft curls, place it just back of your hairline. Comb your own hair over the join, and finish with a silk band. Make use of the hair accessories which are available to decorate, join or jazz up your added hair.

Hair colouring

Whether to tint, dye or colour-rinse the hair is a familiar question in the lives of many women, who for reasons of their own, want to change the colour of their hair. Be the change drastic or subtle, it takes some thought, preparation and information on just what is involved in changing your natural colour, whether permanently or just for a short time.

There was a time when women only 'coloured' their hair to hide the grey – not any more. Women now change the colour of their hair for all kinds of reasons: to highlight the natural colour; to change the look of dull hair; or just to change the shade because it'll be more attractive. The Greeks, Romans and Egyptians dyed their hair to indicate social status. Henna and indigo were most popular among the Persians and Greeks, while the Romans were partial to blonde. They used many of the ingredients that we use today, but they were neither as easy to apply nor as sophisticated as our own modern methods.

What exactly happens to the hair shaft when we change the colour of 'virgin' hair? What is a dye? A tint? Do you want to achieve a permanent colour or just a temporary one? How does a brunette become a redhead? How many kinds of dyes are there? Just start reading labels some day in a department store – it will almost boggle your mind to see the number of bleaches, oils, powders, colour rinses, oxidation dyes, colour shampoos, semi-permanent colours, toners and the rest. You can choose from powders, creams, sprays or liquids; there's something for everybody from the novice to the very adventurous person who is determined to have a new hair colour. What will it be?

Temporary colours (this includes rinses)

These colour only the cuticle (the outer layer) of the hair. They do not effect the hair shaft itself and can be quite useful in improving the look of lifeless hair because they give it highlights. They are fine for pick-ups, but remember that they do shampoo out which means that if you want to maintain the colour you must keep repeating the treatment. They are useful for reviving tinted hair between touch-ups; the result will resemble a permanent colour – but won't last as long.

Colours now come in cans and may be sprayed on – so try a few. They will show you what you might look like with a new colour, or with streaks. They can give you a wonderful party look – and they shampoo out.

Semi-permanent colours

These partially penetrate the hair cuticle just *below* the surface, and so are *in* the hair rather than *on* it. They therefore have a longer lasting result. They have no effect on the natural colour pigment. They are available in either lotions or shampoos. The big difference between semi-permanent and permanent colours is that the semi-permanent ones do not use peroxide or a developer so it is not possible to go from a dark to a light colour. Instead you will be limited to your own hair colour range. Semi-permanent colours last through three to five shampoos.

Permanent colour or tinting is the only way to change the colour of your hair completely. By the use of developers and peroxide the hair shaft is softened and made receptive to colour. The result is permanent and will last until the hair grows out. These dyes or tints compose the largest group of hair colouring products on the market. They are very popular because they are easy to use, whether they pour on or shampoo in. They produce colour that lasts and looks natural, and their versatility is the reason why so many women use them.

What exactly does take place when these oxidation dyes are applied to the hair? A chemical reaction takes place from the mixture of the dye with the developer causing the hair to be stripped and coloured at the same time. This is called the single process method. The liquid has to be left on from fifteen to thirty minutes to give it time to 'develop'. The result is that it is possible to change the hair colour radically in just one step. The effect of the dye is permanent; it will not wash out. The only drawback is that if it is the wrong colour, then you're stuck with it. So be attentive to the colour you choose, read all of the directions on the label and follow instructions for the best results.

Important

- Do a 'patch test' each time you use a dye, because you may have become sensitised since the last time you used it. This simply means that it is quite possible for you to have developed an allergy to the dye which, when used, will cause a severe reaction around your eyes, face and neck.
- Remember to use a conditioner for your type of hair as the repeated use of oxidation dyes (which contain peroxide) will cause some breakage in the hair if it is not conditioned regularly. You should use a protein conditioner after every shampoo and have a twenty-minute heat treatment once a month, especially if your hair is straightened.
- If you relax your hair *and* dye it – wait at least six weeks before you use a dye.
- Use tints manufactured for *black* women.
- Remember, the colour you choose should compliment your skin tone.

Hints for hair problems

- Before colouring or relaxing hair, apply a small amount of any good conditioner to the ends to prevent over-processing.
- Find a styling lotion and neutrilizer that is also a good detangler, and you won't have to use a cream rinse after shampooing. Apply it to your hair, comb through and leave on.
- Plaits? First spray an oil sheen/conditioner on to prevent dry scalp.
- Dry hair? Massage scalp, it aids circulation and prepares scalp for treatment.
- Apply salad cream or mayonnaise (rich in eggs) to the hair. Work it through with your fingers (yes, it's messy, but good!). Don't neglect the ends.
- Wrap your head in a hot towel for fifteen minutes or until cool. Then shampoo carefully until hair is free of the 'treatment'.
- Plaits? Shampoo by popping on a stocking cap. Shampoo and condition, taking care not to pull out extensions, or scratch scalp.
- Very short hair? Try this. Shampoo and condition. While damp apply setting gel. Work through hair. Style.
- Use the spray activator left over from your curly perm to spray on your defrissaged hair. Style softly.
- Shoulder-length natural hair? Thio perm (it gives you *more* control) your hair and roll up in large rollers *or* use brown paper, it's most effective. Brush or comb out and finish with a bit of light hair oil for sheen.

3 Make-up

Egyptian tombs from as long ago as 3,500 BC reveal eye make-up and aromatic ointments, so in a way the wearing of make-up to enhance beauty was an Egyptian and Assyrian innovation, practised by both men and women. This practice had spread to Greece, Rome and the Middle East by the first century AD. While in many African and North American Indian tribes facial decoration was associated with magic and war, some tribes used it for aesthetic purposes, and Africans pioneered the art of hair styling. The Far Eastern countries contributed much to perfumery – the world's finest scents have not always come from Paris.

Everyone wants to be 'beautiful' but, to be sure, great beauties have taken a lot of time and effort to become so. Beauty is ten per cent God-given and ninety per cent hard work. No matter how much make-up and scent you wear, you must be clean

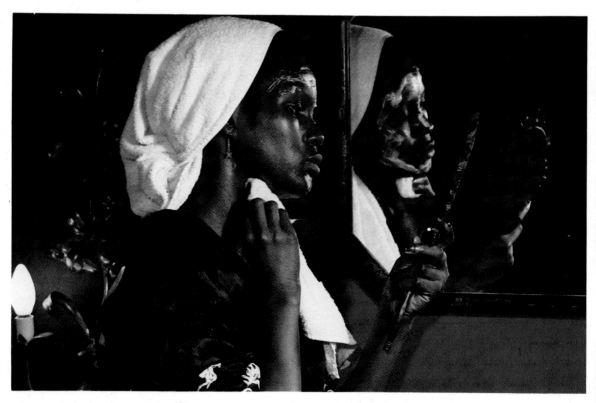

first, from head to toe; your nails must be manicured; your hands, feet and elbows lotioned and smooth; your teeth healthy and shining; and you must concern yourself with the condition of your hair. Of course, inner beauty counts too; who wants to be a pretty rat-bag? But, even more important, what you put into your body in the way of food can determine the way you look and feel. Fatty foods can make blackheads run rampant – and make you fat, sluggish and introverted. (This will be discussed in the diet/exercise section.)

If you have assessed your skin type and developed a skin-care routine, then your clean face (and neck) are ready for you to start work – with a moisturiser first, of course.

Whether or not you make-up or paint your face, and to what degree, depends a great deal upon your lifestyle. Obviously, if you're only popping across the road to get a pint of milk, a dash of lipstick and blusher will suffice. Whatever the occasion, the way you look is as important as the manner in which you behave. Those entering the world of make-up must be adventurous at heart, for there is a great deal of trial and error involved. Be prepared to experiment with different colour combinations and use varied forms of lighting so that you get some perspective of how certain lights affect make-up. Be a bold artist, painting the world's greatest canvas; you can always wipe away what you don't like with a bit of cotton wool and begin again. It also takes practice to draw lines with a steady hand; it sometimes helps to sit with your elbows resting on the dressing table. Eventually, of course, you will get to the stage where you can do it all standing in front of the bathroom mirror, in ten minutes flat.

When you develop a style that suits you, stick to it. Be aware, though, of what is happening around you and be open to new ideas. You should also realise that the most expensive cosmetics are not necessarily always the best; there are many pretty packages for sale that are filled with perfumes and unnecessary additives. Just use common sense and shop around for cosmetics that suit you. If any product irritates your skin, stop using it at once and try something else. It is wise to invest in a good foundation, particularly if your skin is sensitive.

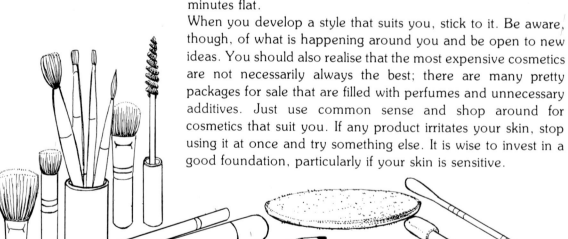

Before you can seriously get down to learning which make-up
suits you best, you have to arm yourself with the tools of the
trade: a good set of make-up brushes; pencils; powder puffs; a
cosmetic sponge or two. There are many brush kits on sale and
the prices range from four to four hundred pounds! You will
need about six to eight basic types of brushes, preferably sable,
and a few assorted sponge-type brushes for powder eye
shadows.

Lighting and its effects

The same make-up will look different in daylight, sunlight, twilight or nightlight. Tricks of light can make older faces look younger or vice versa. Always apply your make-up in the kind of light you'll be seen in. Stick to pastel, almost transparent colours for bright sunshine or summertime. Use a moisturiser or sunscreen, like cocoa butter, instead of a foundation. Artificial light requires stronger make-up. Moisturise, then even the skin tone with foundation. Outline the lips in pencil and dust over lots of loose face powder, more than you need, then brush off the excess. Use a darker shade of blusher around your temples and the hollows of your cheeks. Highlight your eyes, lips and cheekbones with plenty of shine. Don't forget your browbone, the bridge of your nose or the cleft in your chin. If you are going to the disco your make-up should be warm and bright. You'll find that pale greys and browns seem harsh and create hollows under neon lights. Electric light is very even and calls for striking, definite colours, while softly, softly, candlelight is the most flattering light of all.

Modern make-up manufacturers have discovered black beauty and now, more than ever, offer a wide variety of choice for every skin tone. Every woman wants to look stunning and sophisticated; skilfully applied make-up helps to achieve the right result. Some women argue that they don't need make-up and that they want to be 'natural', but perhaps they just need a little confidence in themselves, or maybe they just have never been shown how to wear make-up properly. The self does not have to be sacrificed just because you want to add a little polish, sparkle and shine to your face. Pay no attention to the myth that black women need not wear foundation. Foundation protects the skin from city grime as well as providing a flawless, smooth finish. Water based or oil free foundations are for oily skin types; wear them and you need not worry about your make-up creasing, running or shining in unwanted places. The simplest kind of foundation, which also acts as a moisturiser, is vanishing cream; it is colourless and invisible on the skin.

Moisturisers have two purposes. They protect the skin from environmental pollution and seal in the body's natural moisture, thus the skin is replenished and kept supple. You should never apply foundation or make-up of any kind without first smoothing a moisturiser over your entire face, from the neck upwards.

There are numerous moisturising ingredients from which to choose. Look at the list of ingredients on the label of your moisturiser.

Greases are cocoa butter, hydrogenated oil, lanolin and vaseline.

Oils are avocado, butyl myristate or stearate, cod liver oil, cottonseed oil, dimethicone, grapeseed oil, isopropyl palminate or myristate, mineral oil, mink oil, olive oil, peach-kernel oil, peanut oil, pecan oil, safflower oil, shark-liver oil, squalane, turtle oil and wheat germ oil.

Waxes are beeswax, ceresin, cetyl alcohol, cetyl palmitate, cholesterol, glyceryl stearate, micro-crystalline wax, paraffin, propylene glycol, stearate, sorbitan stearate, stearic acid, stearyl alcohol . . . it's amazing what's going on in all those pretty bottles, tubes and jars.

Hydrolysed animal proteins are milk, oestrogen, pectin, poloxamer, placenta extract, pregnenolone acetate, propylene glycol, royal jelly, sorbitol, yucca and urea.

Non-moisturising ingredients are allantoin, aloe juice, carrageenan, cellulose gum, egg, gelatin, glycerine, hexalene glycol and honey.

Cocoa butter is an excellent moisturiser which is suitable for the entire body. It nourishes and protects the skin and gives it a beautiful shine. Great lashings of baby oil will do, whilst vaseline is one of the best moisturiser/protectants since it has no perfumes, preservatives or irritants.

Even if you have oily skin you need a moisturiser because oil and moisture are not quite the same things. There is a wide variety of oil-free moisturisers on the market, so shop around for what suits you best.

When choosing a foundation, be sure to test it on your inner arm, just above the wrist. Try to assess if the colour suits you in just about any type of lighting. One of the difficulties darker black women have found has been the tendency of foundations to turn whitish-grey and chalky; this can be overcome by mixing an unsuitable colour with a darker one, or by using a darker powder, lightly dusted on top. This should be reason enough for you to use a foundation made for black women. These prevent the shiny look by substituting moisturiser for mineral oil. There

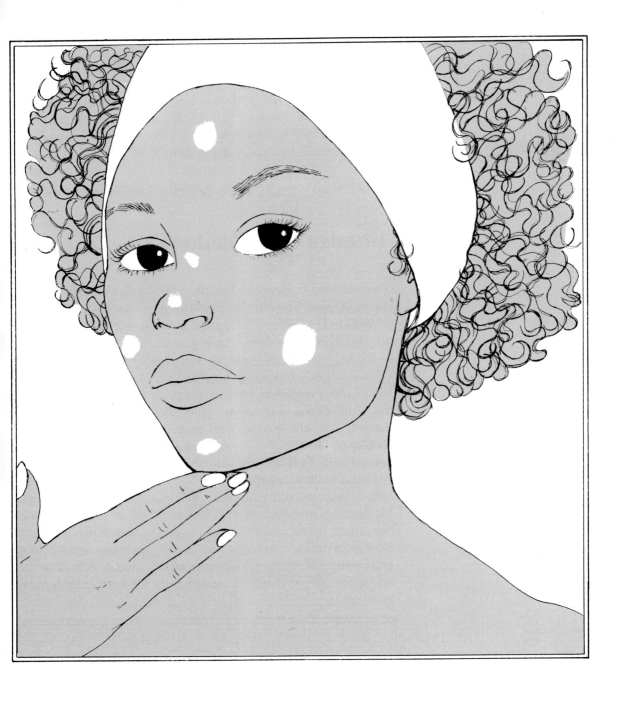

are times when foundations can be used to lighten or shadow certain features, so don't be afraid to experiment. Dot bronzing gels over your forehead as well as on your cheekbones and throat, blending upwards, always.

Whenever foundation is worn during the day, only the smallest amount is necessary. Save the heavy foundation for discotheques; even then, don't go overboard, you don't want to look painted or as if you're wearing a mask.

How to apply foundation

If you use a liquid foundation, dot a small amount on your forehead, nose, cheeks, chin and throat. Then blend it in using upward strokes, making sure that the colour spreads and that your eyebrows are not clogged with it. If you use a pressed powder or creme type foundation, this also applies. Blend in with either your fingertips or a damp cosmetic sponge.

'Shades of perfection'

You will want to develop shading techniques, depending on the shape of your face and the features you want to emphasise or minimise. The first rule is never to paint, smear or rub on make-up. Dot it on with a light, stippling touch, then blend and feather it so that there will be no harsh and obvious lines. This is where your soft bristled make-up brushes come in.

When using a blusher, or rouge, cover just the highest part of the cheekbones with colour and shade in with a brush or natural, cosmetic sponge. Feel your cheekbone or suck in your cheeks to identify the 'blush' area. Blend out the edges for a natural look. Darker skins look fantastic in plums, purples, bright reds and mellow oranges. Shy away from brown blushers; they only fade away into your skin, dulling it instead of adorning it. Medium to light brown skins are stunning in shades of rose, burgundy, russet and tangerine. Experiment with two shades of blusher, a darker one in the hollows of the cheeks and a lighter, brighter one lifting the cheekbones and forehead. A blusher that shimmers with gold can be shaded on to the ears, chin, temples and throat.

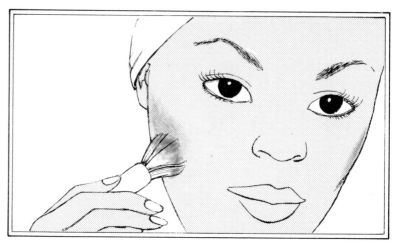

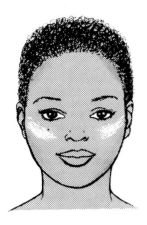

If you have a round face, learn to contour the cheeks, forehead and chin to create the illusion of thinness. Place a cream, liquid or powder two shades darker than your foundation under the cheekbones and blend to the outer edges of your cheeks from ear to chin. Highlight the tops of your cheeks with a frosted powder. You can add to this illusion by drawing angular lines on your cheekbones before putting on your foundation base.

A square face has hard, angular lines which need softening, so gently shade the entire jawline and temple area around the hairline with a tone two shades darker than your foundation to give your face a rounder look. Add warmth with fiery or cinnamon blush on the throat, tips of the ears, and under the chin.

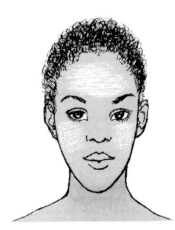

A long face is made to look more symmetrical by smoothing a lighter foundation over your cheeks and forehead, then a darker foundation over your chin and neck. A long nose is shortened by smoothing a darker base just under the tip and a broad nose can be narrowed by blending a light line of make-up down the centre and a darker base along each side. A bronze or gold gleam from the centre of the forehead, down the centre of the nose, also gives a fine, sculpted shape to a broad nose.

If your chin recedes, blend in a lighter shade of foundation on your chin, just in the centre, or dust with an iridescent blusher. If your chin protrudes, blend in a darker shade of foundation, just at the tip.

For a diamond-shaped face, soften the angles by using a shade two tones darker than your normal foundation on the highest part of the forehead and tip of the chin. Highlight the sides of your forehead and jawline with a shade two tones lighter than your foundation, or with a gold gleamer. Accent eyes and play up your cheekbones.

Give curves to a triangular face by highlighting the temples and the tip of the chin with a shade two tones lighter than your foundation. Contour the top of the forehead with a shade two tones darker than your foundation, just along the hairline. Slightly darken the area just beneath the jawline and the ears. The hairstyle that you choose should also make the most of your face. Triangular faces need a hairstyle that gives width and softness to the forehead and covers the outermost part of the jawline.

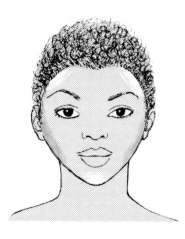

The heart-shaped face needs shading on the temples and on the tip of the chin with two tones lighter than your foundation. Highlight the outer jawline with a shade two tones darker than your foundation, or gold gleamer to brighten up your cheeks.

An oval or egg-shaped face is considered symmetrically correct and is the ideal shape. Your face only needs a minimum of contouring and shading. You can, however, make use of shading techniques to play up certain features, as the mood takes you.

If you wish to set make-up for the whole day, use a puff full of fine, transluscent powder and press it firmly, without rubbing, all over your face, including brows and lids. Brush off excess with a soft brush or clean cotton wool. Alternatively, fill a large brush with powder and dust on horizontally, then brush off gently, using vertical strokes. To set make-up and prevent smudging without powdering, press a cold, damp sponge over your entire face or pat the face with a dry washcloth filled with crushed ice. Many an appearance has been spoilt by sloppy eye shadow, or for that matter, the lack of it. If your face is made up and your eyes are bare, your face looks unbalanced – even a gold shine over the lids is better than nothing at all. Dull, tired eyes mean that you are not getting enough sleep. Eyes should be bright and clear and, though it's okay to use eyedrops once in a while, you shouldn't make a habit of it. A quick exercise can relieve eyestrain:

Roll your eyes up, to the left, down and to the right; close eyes and roll in a circular motion, open and repeat rotation in opposite direction.

For laugh lines or 'bags' under the eyes, dot a white stick or a blemish erasing stick just beneath your lower lashes from the inside of your nose to the far corner of your eye. Do this both before and after applying foundation, then blend in gently with the fingertips or a small sponge-type brush. A gold stick or gold dust also lighten under-eye shadows.

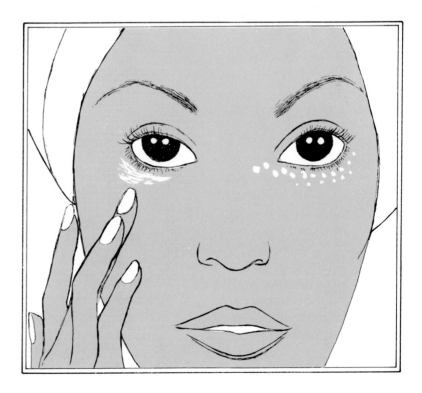

You can also minimise under-eye shadows by using dark grey or blue eye shadow on lids, blending subtly and extending it up to your brows. Deepen the crease of the lid by carefully drawing a line, following the natural line of the crease, with a sharp, repeat sharp, brown pencil. 'Set' the line with a deep, bright powder shadow and fade up into the brow bone. Dot a white, gold or bronze shine just beneath the eyebrows, using slightly more at the sides of the eyes, where the brows end. Blend in gently, always following the browline.

Draw a line at the roots of your lashes with a soft, bright blue or black pencil to make your eyes look clearer and brighter.

There are three basic types of eyeliner

Make-up liquid, which is used mostly for stage, pencil and cake eyeliner.

- Pencils are much more popular these days; they come in delightful colours so that you are no longer limited to black or brown.
- Cake eyeliner has the slight edge over pencil in that it does not run so easily, but it does need an adept hand to master its use. Try it, it's economical and the brush work will stand you in good stead for other things.
- Use pencil either over or under powder to eliminate smudges and runs in the creases.

Eyeliner is applied from the inside corner of the eye to the far corner; from there the line can either be extended outward or slanted up or down. If, however, you have heavy eyelids or deep creases that overhang at the outer corner, do not extend the eyeliner beyond the corner of the eye unless you want to look older! If you have a small eye-lid, draw a very thin line along the lash line, widening only at the very corner of the eye. Avoid white, light blue or yellowish shadows unless they are blended to highlight something darker. As a rule, white lids do not flatter black skins.

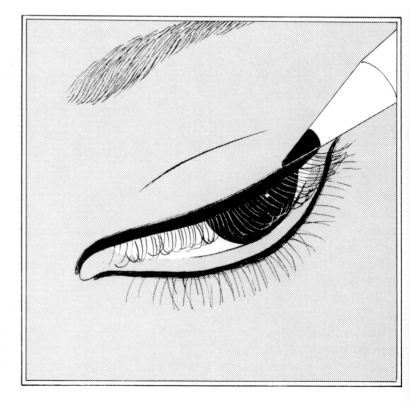

The trick of eyeshadow is exactly that: shading to give a wide-eyed, smoulderly look. Choose a colour that matches your outfit, draw a line and smudge it over your eyelid, adding colour in the corners and creases. Then go for a contrast with a lighter colour under the brows, to heighten the brow bone; possibly a pearly pink. If you do use pink under your eyes and on your cheekbones, blend it lightly – you want it to be seen.

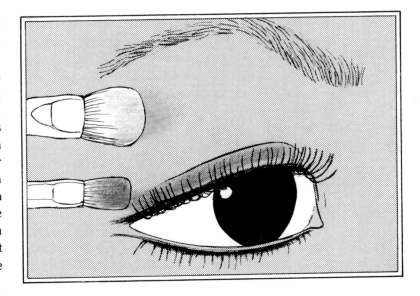

Beige and brown shading can be used to deepen the eye before adding royal blue or a deep, rich green. Don't be afraid of colours; when beautifully applied they're exciting and a pleasure to behold. Smudge eyeliner slightly before it sets to get a softer look.

Mascara comes in cake or liquid form and makes lashes look longer and thicker. There are hypo-allergenic types for sensitive eyes but if you're not keen on mascara at all, try coating the lashes with petroleum jelly.

If you use mascara, fill the brush with it and tip the ends of your lashes, top and bottom. Then cover the rest of the lashes from base to tip, slowly, keeping each lash separate. Dust the lashes lightly with powder and apply another coat of mascara, again slowly from the base to the tip. If the lashes stick together, use a tiny brush to flick them apart gently. Make sure that mascara dries without leaving little dots on your skin. Try blue or green mascara to add another dimension to eye colour.

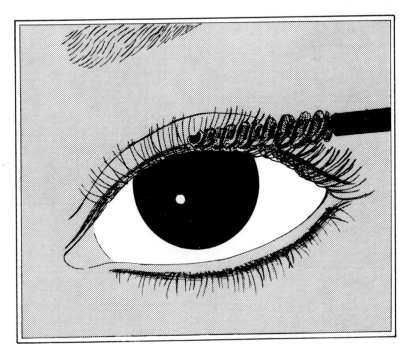

Eyebrows should look as natural as possible; tweeze them only if they are too bushy and straggly. This may take time and practice, so be patient. They can also be made to look thinner by brushing them up from the bottom and down from the top, pinching them together with your fingers. A touch of petroleum jelly will keep them in line.

If you decide to tweeze your brows, it's best to do it immediately after a sauna or facial because the hair comes out of open pores more readily. Pluck only the hair below the arch and follow the natural grain of the hair, otherwise you'll end up with ingrown hairs. After tweezing, apply an astringent, antiseptic or witch-hazel with cotton wool.

If you want to make the most of your natural browline, try this to find its shape. Draw an imaginary line from the widest part of your nose up to your hairline. The brow should begin where the line crosses the hairs of the eyebrow. Draw another, slightly diagonal line from the outer corners of your eye across your temple to the upper edge of your ear to find where the brow should end. Make a pencil dot as your guide. If you imagine a straight, level line from the outer tip of the right brow to the outer tip of the left, then both inner tips should also evenly touch the line.

Eyebrow pencils should be well sharpened – you can use an emery board for this; try filing it into a screwdriver-type shape. If you don't have an eyebrow brush in your kit, brush brows into shape with a children's tooth brush then *PENCIL* in short, feathery strokes, following the natural shape of the brow as closely as possible. Apply from the lower hair upwards, because downward lines will give you a depressed look. Smooth in colour with your fingertip or a cotton swab, or brush with a dry eyelash brush.

To make small eyes look larger, build up brows a bit on top and clear out straggly hairs underneath the arch. Bring out deep-set eyes by enlarging the space between eyes and brows and raise

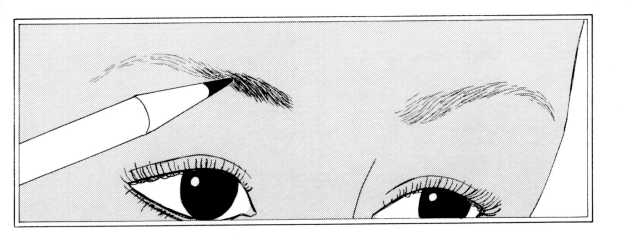

slightly by pencilling in above the line. Eyes too close together can be widened by plucking the space between brows and extending pencil line at ends. Eyes too far apart need pencilling closer to the nose but do not extend the line out at ends.

If your eyes are too prominent, use darker foundation on the lids and darker eyeshadow shades.

For a more natural look, use two shades of eyebrow pencil – dark brown and black, or light and dark brown, black and grey. To set eyebrow make-up for the day, lightly powder over the first application of pencil, using translucent powder, then reapply pencil with feather strokes.

Remove eye make-up and mascara every night with baby oil or your favourite brand of eye make-up removal pads. Apply baby oil with your fingertips and leave it on for a few minutes; then wash with remover or baby soap and water. Rinse, then reapply baby oil to prevent lashes from breaking off.
To reduce and relieve eye puffiness, apply cotton wool pads wrung out in a solution of one pint of hot water and one table-spoonful of salt. Relax with eyes closed and let pads remain on lids for five or more minutes. Rinse with cold water. You can also relax with a warm, damp flannel on your lids for ten minutes, or paint the swollen area with egg white.

Never share eye make-up as infections can result. It is a good idea to sterilise your tweezers before plucking brows, just to be on the safe side. Spectacle wearers should wear somewhat heavier liner, shadow and mascara behind their lenses. Intensify your eyes with liner on both your lower and upper lids, and choose colours which match or compliment your spectacle frames, as well as the colour of your eyes.

Applying lipstick

Always apply lipstick with a brush and begin by outlining your lips in either a darker shade of lipstick or a brown pencil. Try dark grey powder eyeshadow for a stunning effect under red lipstick – the powder also helps the lipstick to adhere longer.

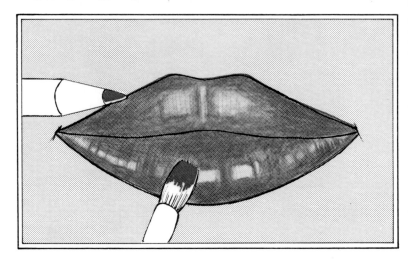

Lips too full? Draw a line just inside your natural lipline, making sure that you have covered your natural lipline with a lighter foundation, thus masking it. Work the brush into the lipstick, cover it with colour and twist it to a point. Then, using short brush strokes, spread the colour evenly on the lips, just inside the line you have drawn. Blend colour so that the line is no more than a subtle shadow.

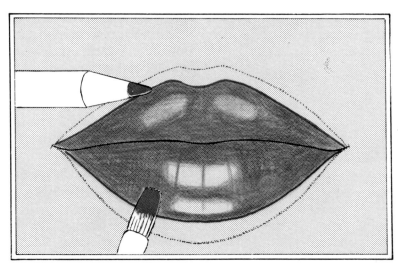

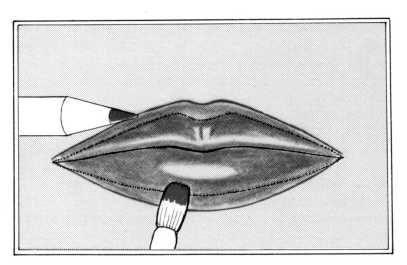

Another way to disguise a too full lip is to use a slightly darker shade of lipstick on the outer lip and dot a lighter gleamer, or gloss, right in the centre.

Lips too thin? Outline them with a brown eyebrow pencil to make them seem fuller, then fill in with lipstick colour.

Experiment with various combinations of lip colour; don't be afraid to blend a lighter tone with a darker to get a desired shade. Your lipstick should always compliment your clothing and nail colour, as well as the rest of your make-up.

Make-up for the mature woman

It is possible to grow old beautifully, gracefully and with dignity. Women of all ages should take care of their bodies and make the most of their appearances.

Older women should veer towards a translucent, matt type finish for powder and foundation, saving high shine for eyes and cheekbones. Bronzes, golds, burgundies and pearly plums look beautiful blended over paler purples, pinks and peach.

Russet or red tinted rouges, clear, creme or powder, are dusted on in a pork chop shape, contouring the jawline; dust off excess with puff, sponge or brush so that colour is never garish.

Lip colour should be bright, but not brassy. Some older women can get away with rich reds, so don't feel as if your lipstick has to be invisible. Unless your skin is a very pale shade of black, don't wear pink lipstick unless it's a hot, hot pink or magenta one.

Also remember that older ladies are not exempt from exercise. No excuses, get busy stretching and toning; you'll be better for it.

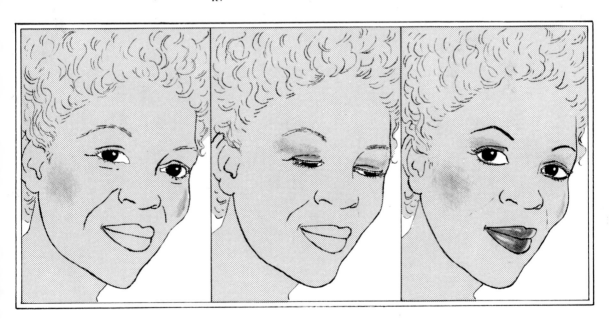

Avoid synthetics like nylon, polyester, crimplene, etc which are used to make drip-dry fabrics. Natural fabrics like cotton, wool and silk let the skin breathe.

You *can* do it – the quickie make-up

Begin with a clean, moisturised face. Using a damp sponge, apply foundation to your face, eyes and lips. Blot with a tissue.

With your largest powder brush, brush lots of translucent powder on to your face (for a matt finish).

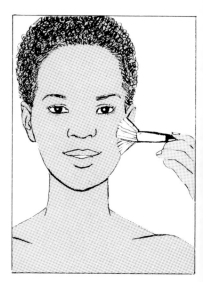

Define your eyes, top and bottom with your thinnest eye pencil. Follow the natural line of your eye.

Highlight your eyes with a sweep of eye-shadow. Use sponge tip or brush. Use a soft colour for day and sparkles for evening.

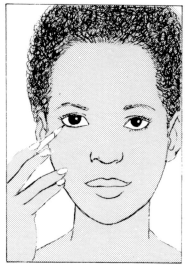

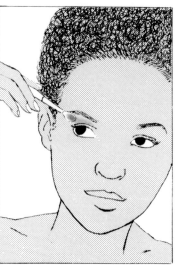

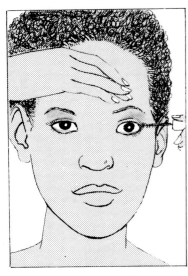

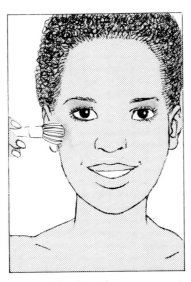

After giving your lashes a coat of loose powder, apply some mascara. Separate your lashes with a brush for a natural look.

Smile. That's where to put your blusher. (Never put it below your nose.)

Brush (down) your entire face to remove any excess powder.

Apply lipstick or lip gloss with a brush.

Use a soft brown pencil on your eyebrows.

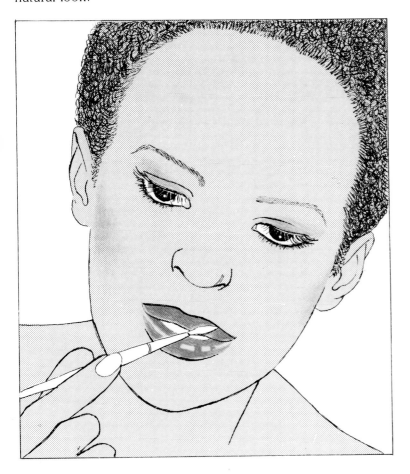

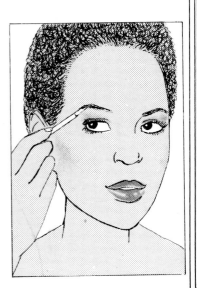

If you ever run out of an essential item, don't panic
Check the bathroom or kitchen cupboard to see if you can make your own substitute.
- Instead of cleansing lotion, use baby soap and water or baby lotion and water.
- Vaseline goes a long way as hair oil, moisturiser and polish for patent leather shoes.
- Home-made foundation is a mixture of two parts face powder and one part moisturiser/white hand lotion (add power to lotion), but this must be used quickly because it deteriorates and spoils. You will find that even the most 'natural' cosmetics have some sort of preservative to discourage bacterial growth.

It's always best to make-up before you dress; many a favourite outfit has been ruined by spilt mascara. After making-up, wash your hands so you don't get smudged fingermarks on your clothes. Always pop a tissue between your lips before pulling your dress over your head.

A great mask or two . . .

Almond cleanser (for oily skin)

½ cup oil of sweet almonds
½ cup powdered oatmeal
½ cup grated pure soap
Mix the ingredients together and place in an airtight jar. Take out a handful and mix with enough water to allow you to rub it on your face when cleansing. Rinse well.

Mint cleanser (stimulates sluggish skin)

2 teaspoonsful of coconut oil
1 teaspoonful of mint infusion (made by steeping 1 oz mint in
    1 pint of boiling water, overnight)
1 drop of cider vinegar
Just melt the coconut oil, add the mint and vinegar and shake well. Apply with cotton wool and don't wash off.

Honey cleansing lotion (for any skin type)

1 teaspoonful of honey
2 tablespoonsful of warm milk
Blend together to make a lotion then rub it over the face and neck with fingertips. Leave for five minutes, rub off, rinse.

Violet skin freshener (for every skin type)

1 tablespoonful of violet flowers
1 cup of cold water
Chop the violet flowers and place them in a pan with the water. Bring to the boil, then simmer for about two minutes. Steep until cold, strain and bottle. Apply to the face with cotton wool and leave to dry.

Wheat germ mask (for all skin types)

1 egg yolk
½ teaspoonful of wheat germ
¾ cup of oil of sweet almonds
1 teaspoonful of distilled water
Beat the first three ingredients together, add the water, beat again. Brush on the face, leave for twenty minutes, then wash off. Do not keep this, it's best made fresh.

Avocado moisturiser (for any skin)

2 eggs
1 teaspoonful of glycerine
½ teaspoonful of lemon juice
2 teaspoonsful of avocado oil
2 egg yolks, beaten
½ teaspoonful of cider vinegar
2 tablespoonsful of distilled water
Mix the eggs, glycerine and lemon juice, then slowly add enough avocado oil to thicken to a cream-like consistency. Stir in the vinegar. Add the beaten egg yolks and water, mixing slowly all the time. Keep refrigerated and rub a small amount on the face and neck morning and night.

Handcare

Take a good look at your hands and observe what impression they give; Sherlock Holmes had only to look at a woman's hands to discover her occupation and her mental state. If you bite your nails you will certainly be put off by the taste of nail varnish, so cover nails and keep them covered, no matter how short. If time or finance won't allow for professional manicures, give yourself an hour a week at home.

Nails grow from the fold of skin at the base of the nail.

As with hair and skin, the part of the nail that we see is dead and is formed from the protein keratin. The lining portion of the nail is buried deeper than the half moon shape at the base. Nail biting, apart from being unsightly, does not damage the nails but they will grow about twice as fast as normal.

Your nails – all you need to know

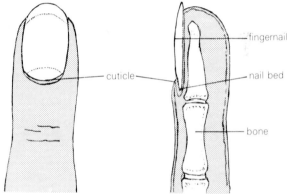

cuticle

fingernail

nail bed

bone

A cross section of your finger

There is no medical evidence to support the view that extra vitamins or minerals in your diet will improve the strength of your nails or prevent them splitting. A balanced diet is all-important however.

Nails

Of course, diet has a lot to do with the strength of nails, so be sure to include protein-rich foods in every meal. Cuticles are the areas of skin, immediately surrounding the nails, which harden as the skin dies. Cuticles must be kept soft and pushed back to enable the nail to breathe and grow.

How to manicure

- Before you begin your manicure, remove all traces of nail varnish and wash your hands.

- Fill a small basin with a dash of olive oil and hot water or washing up liquid and hot water.

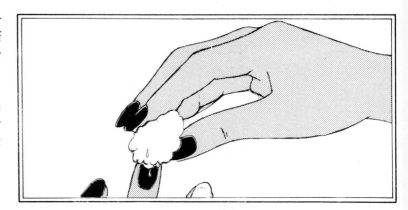

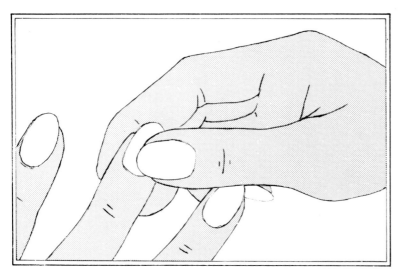

- Soak nails for five minutes, dry them and then rub on cuticle cream or more oil.

- Lift the cuticles and push back with your orange stick and trim any ragged nails with scissors.

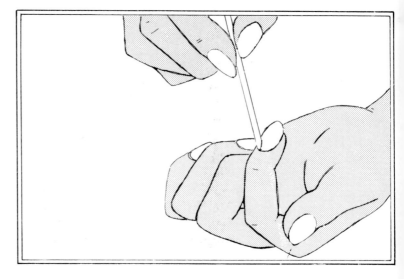

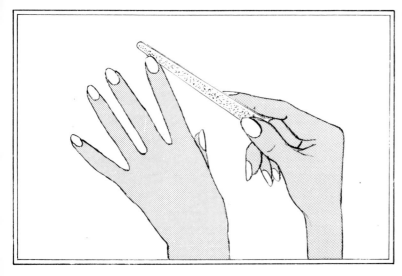

- File nails using the fine side of your emery board and make sure you file in one direction only, towards nail tips.

- Resoak hands, then brush or buff in one direction, twenty or thirty strokes.

- Varnish or polish is optional, but if you use it, first apply a base coat. When that is dry, put on two coats of varnish and seal with a top coat, then gently press the very tips of nails to help prevent polish from chipping at the ends.

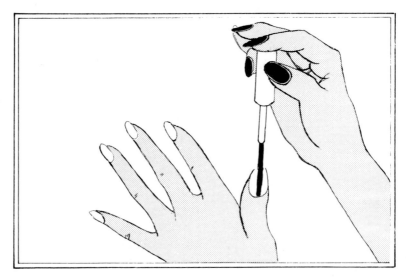

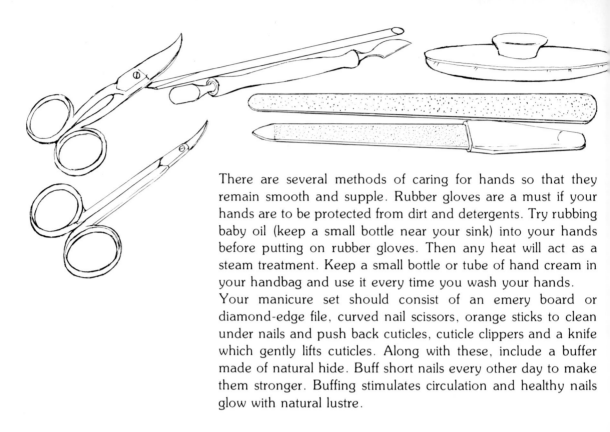

There are several methods of caring for hands so that they remain smooth and supple. Rubber gloves are a must if your hands are to be protected from dirt and detergents. Try rubbing baby oil (keep a small bottle near your sink) into your hands before putting on rubber gloves. Then any heat will act as a steam treatment. Keep a small bottle or tube of hand cream in your handbag and use it every time you wash your hands.

Your manicure set should consist of an emery board or diamond-edge file, curved nail scissors, orange sticks to clean under nails and push back cuticles, cuticle clippers and a knife which gently lifts cuticles. Along with these, include a buffer made of natural hide. Buff short nails every other day to make them stronger. Buffing stimulates circulation and healthy nails glow with natural lustre.

Feet fit for a queen

In your haste to get up and go make sure that you're really well-groomed from head to toe. Even if you remember to lotion or oil your feet, you might squeeze them into shoes which are too tight, too high or too pointed. Apart from high heels throwing your body off-balance, tight, cramped shoes cause poor circulation, blisters, corns, callouses and bunions. Feet should never be neglected; they deserve regular attention and need plenty of air and exercise.

It's always a mistake to buy shoes without first trying them on, and it's not a good idea to wear other people's shoes. Feet should be measured regularly because their size can change — for instance, if you've gained weight, your feet will be broader. Feet can also broaden if you change jobs and do more walking. When you buy shoes, make sure they are comfortable; they should grip firmly at the heel and be long enough and wide enough. Don't kid yourself that a too-tight shoe will stretch — they never do. There's no real need for you to walk or hobble around in misery. If you buy sling-backs, check that when the strap is adjusted your heel is resting on the platform of the heel, not spreading over it at the back or sides.

Rest shoes by wearing them on alternate days and air shoes before putting shoe trees in them. Dry out wet shoes slowly, keeping toes in shape with trees or rolled-up newspaper. Clean shoes often and have them repaired regularly – down at heel shoes look tacky and are bad for your posture.

Any heels over two inches upset the shock-absorbing function of your arches. The arches provide graceful movement and bear the weight of your body; toes are for strength and balance. If you're one of those who are tottering around, tripping over and twisting ankles in high heels, ask yourself why. The way your body is balanced determines good posture and good health. Pregnant women especially should avoid high heels. The extra weight you carry, combined with high heels, can really damage your pelvis and spine.

Feet, like the rest of your body, should be washed daily. Dry carefully, especially between the toes and rub in baby oil or hand lotion.

Give yourself a pedicure every fortnight.

First, soak feet in warm, soapy water for twenty minutes to soften skin. You can also soak in bath oil of some kind.

Gently rub any callouses so that they absorb the water then carefully push back cuticles with an orange stick or cotton bud (Q-tip). Don't clip, scrape or dig at the cuticle. Do remove callouses with a pumice stone.

To clip your nails, cut straight across so that you do not injure the delicate tissue down the sides.

Buff each nail and massage the feet with moisturiser or baby oil. Remove all traces of oil from toenails before putting on nail polish.

To relieve hot, tired feet, soak feet in lukewarm water with sliced lemon for twenty minutes.

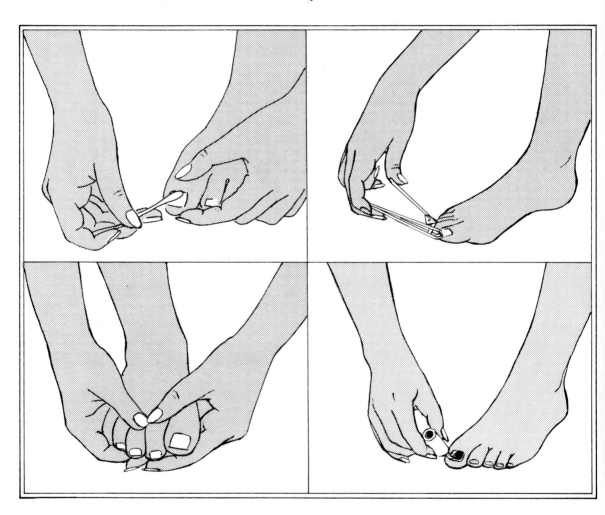

What's so secret about secret ingredients?

Emulsifiers: enable non-mixable ingredients to blend smoothly and stay that way.

Solvents: make products dissolve.

Lanolin: is an emollient, emulsifier and a base used in cleansing lotions.

Powders: made mostly of kaolin, talc, zinc oxide, titanium oxide, zinc stearate and chalk.

Cake make-up: powder is mixed with dry gum, (gum tragacanth), sodium alginate or carboxymethyl cellulose. Hot water is added and the mixture is stirred until gum dissolves and dries.

Liquid make-up: suspensions, ie powder mixed into a liquid medium, either water or oil.

Sticks: lipstick, mascara, pencils are generally made of castor oil and beeswax with ozokerite (hydrocarbon wax) acting as stiffening agents.

Vanishing creams: are oil in water emulsions which penetrate the skin without leaving oil surface film.

Emulsions: consist of two liquids that do not dissolve in each other. There are two types.
1) Oil in water: fine particles of water dispersed in fat or oil with the aid of an emulsifier, whose type depends on end product.
2) Water in oil; fine particles of oil dispersed in water. Most creams and lotions are emulsions but lotions have a higher water content than creams.

Nail polish: is nitrocellulose lacquer with a plasticiser to make it spread. Guanine, or extract of fish scales, is what gives polish a frosted look.

4 Diet

is not a dirty word

In the dictionary, diet is defined as the kind of food on which a person lives; it is a food regimen. It is not a crash course in calorie reduction from a May issue of a magazine and it is not something harsh beyond human control. Diet is *not* a dirty word.

Psychological eating problems are almost exclusive to women; they range from anorexia nervosa to compulsive eating/dieting. Somehow, food has become tangled up in a system of self-denial and reward, when in fact it should be seen as what it is: fuel for the body.

Anorexia is compulsive self-starvation, which is not about being the right weight. The desire to be slim becomes obsessive to the point where anorexics can no longer see how skinny and emaciated they have become; to themselves, they look fat.

On the other hand, many people seek solace in food. A few slices of cheesecake are taken for depression, and so on. This is okay as long as you remain in control. Most important, obesity is caused by a poor diet as well as over-eating. What you put into your body will show on you in some way or another; a good nutritional diet is not a drag. That you will look better and perhaps feel more confident is incidental; you will be in good health.

The basic body requirements are carbohydrates (sugars and starches), fats, proteins, vitamins and minerals (including trace elements). Carbohydrates and fats supply energy, proteins supply the material for growth, while vitamins and minerals regulate body functions.

Carbohydrates

Starches are converted into *sugars* when broken down by digestion so they pose a minor threat to the waistline. Refined foods should be avoided at all costs: white sugar, white flour and white rice have been stripped of nutritional values, notably the group B vitamins. Refined sugar encourages tooth decay. Brown rice has five times the niacin (vitamin PP), eight times the thiamine (vitamin B_1) and three times the riboflavin (vitamin B_2) of boiled white rice. The same sort of figures apply to brown or whole wheat breads, pastas and sugar.

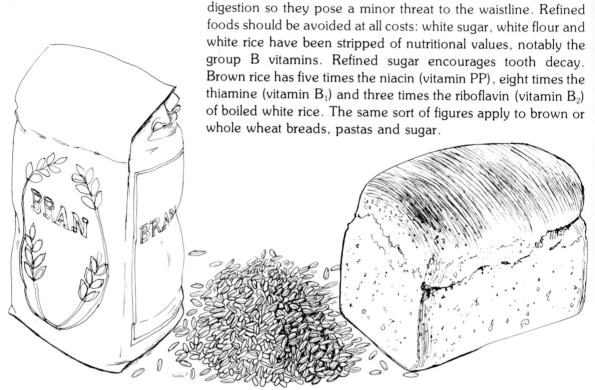

Root vegetables are another important source of carbohydrates. Chips or french-fries are high in calories because they have been fried whereas a serving of baked or boiled potatoes has only 100 calories. It is wise to eat the skin of the potato as this will increase your intake of vitamin C. Mashing potatoes halves the mineral content and destroys some vitamins.

Fats

Fats are divided into two categories: saturated and unsaturated. Saturated fats are mostly solid at room temperature and include animal fats, solid vegetable shortenings, and coconut and palm kernel oils; unsaturated or polyunsaturated fats are oils which are liquid at room temperature and include vegetable oils and fish oils. Sixty per cent of the calories in red meat come from saturated fats, so grill meat until well done.

Cholesterol resembles fat and is essential, but only in small quantities. A high level of cholesterol is linked with heart disease and high blood pressure. Eggs contain a lot of cholesterol. Vegetable fats can be substituted for animal fats to lower cholesterol levels, but low fat diets restrict both animal and vegetable fats. Visible fats are lard, butter and fat on meat, while invisible fats are found in nuts, mackerel, salmon and pork. Avocadoes are the richest source of polyunsaturated oils for the vegetarian.

Proteins

Proteins, the body builders, are made up of chains of amino acids, crucial for growth and repair of tissues. Good sources of protein are milk foods, soya beans, wheat germ, nuts, fish, meat, and pulses and beans (red kidney beans, black-eyed peas, split peas, chick peas, butter beans, aduki beans and lentils).

Cooked together, brown rice and beans or whole wheat macaroni and cheese are complete sources of protein. Beans and pulses have a low calorie content, high roughage content and the lowest fat content of any of the protein foods. Always include roughage in your diet to prevent constipation. Other valuable sources of roughage are fruits, whole grains and whole cereals.

An imbalanced diet invariably leads to loss of health and symptoms of vitamin deficiencies; you become what you eat, so eat well.

Be aware that you function and look best with a healthy diet and develop an interest in this. Read the labels of packaged foods to know which are worth eating. The natural vitamins and minerals are worth eating – not the additives and white sugar. There is really no need for anyone to require a set of dentures in his or her lifetime. Certainly 'bad' eating habits won't disappear overnight, but the more aware you are of what is good for you the better your capacity for discrimination, and then elimination, of junk foods that clog your system. Invest in a good cook-book, or two – be really daring and try vegetarian recipes, just to see what you might be missing.

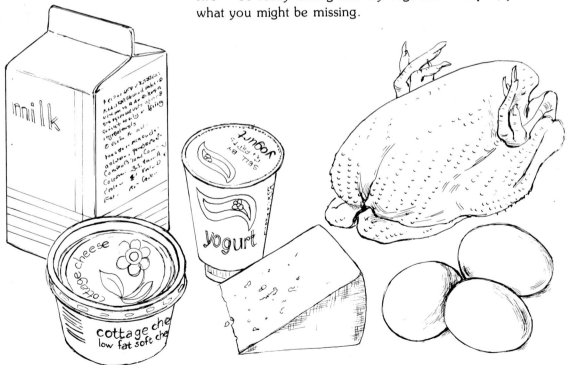

Vitamins

Vitamins were not discovered until 1901, but they have been used to prevent and cure disease since 1754 when a British naval surgeon said he believed that scurvy, a serious ailment affecting sailors on long voyages, was due to lack of something in their diets. He suggested a daily ration of lime juice, which saved countless lives and resulted in British sailors acquiring the nickname 'limeys'. The dietary deficiency proved to be a lack of vitamin C. Vitamins also prevent other deficiency diseases, such as rickets, beriberi and pellegra; they prevent anaemia and infections; they aid blood clotting on the surface of the skin, release of energy from carbohydrates and absorption of minerals.

Vitamin A is important for healthy skin and eyes. Sources of vitamin A are: carrots, green leafy vegetables, sweet potatoes, liver, egg yolks, prunes, apricots, butter and corn-on-(or off!) the-cob. The vitamin A in fruits and vegetables is in a form called carotene and has to be converted to vitamin A (retinol), in your body. It was given the name carotene because it was first identified in the yellow pigment of carrots. If you lack vitamin A, your eyes cannot adapt to changes in light and night-blindness occurs. Other disorders of the eye develop when this vitamin is absent from your diet and your skin becomes dry and less resistant to infection. Asparagus, broccoli, collard/dandelion/mustard/or turnip greens, and squash or marrow also come high on the list of rich sources of vitamin A.

Vitamin B_1, Thiamine, is important for good digestion and utilisation of sugars. Sources are rice, peas, broad beans, brazil nuts, yeast products (of which Marmite is one), whole grain flours, wheat germ and molasses.

Vitamin B_2, Riboflavin, is important for healthy skin, good eyesight, muscle growth and tone. Sources are liver, beans, avocado, soya bean flour, kidneys, heart and cocoa.

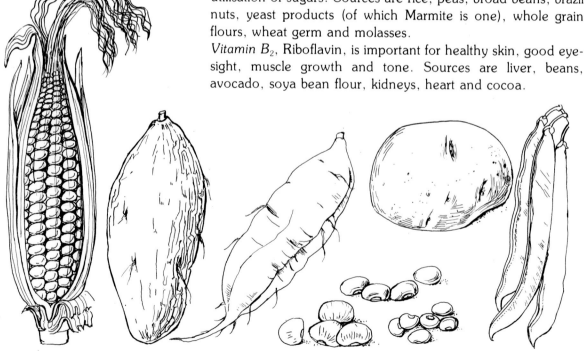

Vitamin PP, Niacin, or *Nicotinic acid,* is vital for good skin and it prevents diarrhoea and mental disorders. Sources are wheat, liver, meat and poultry, bran, prunes and peaches.

Vitamin B$_5$, Pantothenic acid, is essential for making you feel full of energy. Sources are whole grain products, liver, eggs, yeast, kidney, royal jelly and fresh vegetables. All vitamins are destroyed by excessive heat, and treatment with alkalis. Vitamin deficiencies are most likely to arise from excessive intake of refined foods.

Pyridoxine, or *vitamin B$_6$,* is found in liver, wheat germ, eggs, green vegetables and yeast products; it is vital for amino acid metabolism and thus protein formation.

Vitamin B$_{12}$, Cyanocobalamin, has a relationship with folic acid in the formation of red blood cells and also maintains a healthy nervous system. Sources are red meats, liver and kidney, fish and dairy products. Vegans (people who eat neither meat nor dairy produce) should beware they do not lack B$_{12}$.

Folic acid is found in pulses, raw, green leafy vegetables, fruit and liver. This vitamin is usually lost in cooking water, canning processes or prolonged heating of foods. Deficiencies may also be induced by pregnancy or contraceptive pills.

Biotin is found in liver, kidney, yeast extract, cauliflower, nuts and pulses. It is vital to production of fatty acids and for the release of energy from food.

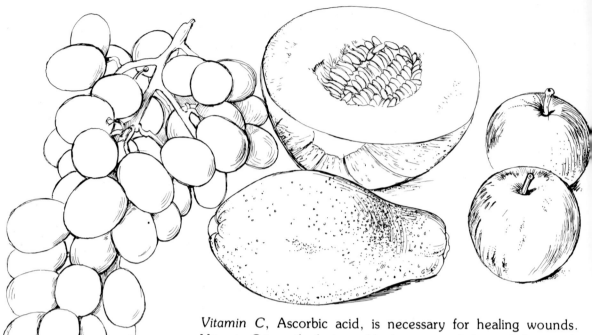

Vitamin C, Ascorbic acid, is necessary for healing wounds. Vitamin C is easily destroyed by heat or sunlight, and along with all the B complex vitamins, is water soluble, so don't throw away cooking water, or all the vitamins will be lost. Sources are citrus fruits, rose hips, green vegetables, potatoes, tomatoes and cantaloupe melons.

Vitamin D, essential for good bone structure, prevents tooth decay. Sources are eggs, milk, butter, liver and fish oils. Even walking in the sunshine is a good source of vitamin D. This vitamin is formed in the skin in sunlight. Without this vitamin, the body cannot absorb calcium and phosphorus from food.

Vitamin E, Tocopherol, is a vitamin found in wheat germ, safflower oil, pure vegetable oils, leafy vegetables and whole grains. Vitamin E is stored throughout the body, especially in fat. Commercially synthesised or chemically produced vitamin E is used as an antioxidant to retard food spoilage. In your body, vitamin E from the above food sources protects vitamin A and cells from destructive oxidation by slowing down the process. Lack of vitamin E causes muscle fibres to break down and stiffen. Vitamin E soothes and heals the skin.

Vitamin K can be found in cauliflower, cabbage, spinach, peas and foods produced from cereal grains. It is fat soluble, as are vitamins A, D and E. It is important for clotting blood at the site of wounds.

Miso is fermented soya bean purée which contains living enzymes. Miso also provides a nutritious balance of essential oils, minerals, carbohydrates, vitamins and protein. Never boil miso. Two other main types are mugi, made from barley, and genmai, made from brown rice. All are a source of B_{12}.

Minerals

Minerals, like vitamins, are also essential factors in a well balanced diet. Sodium, magnesium, calcium and potassium are some of the most highly concentrated minerals present in the body, therefore it is imperative that your daily intake of these from vegetable sources is high. Trace elements, such as iron, manganese, cobalt, copper, zinc, molybdenum, iodine and selenium are not needed in great quantities but are just as essential; an iron deficiency, for instance, could lead to anaemia.

Salt, or *sodium chloride*, is the most common mineral found in foods and salt deficiencies usually arise from excessive loss through perspiration, particularly if you do hard, physical work in a hot climate. It is not really necessary to add salt to food; a normal, varied diet is ample for most requirements. Too much salt intake can be dangerous especially to babies as their kidneys are not equipped to excrete the excess, so never add salt to their diets. Some foods are processed with high salt concentrations: canned vegetables, crisps and salted meats are but a few.

Calcium is a must for healthy bones and teeth; it is found in milk foods, green vegetables and eggs.

Phosphorus, like calcium, is needed to build membranes of cells, bones and teeth. If you have enough protein and calcium you will automatically get enough phosphorus, because it is found in the same foods.

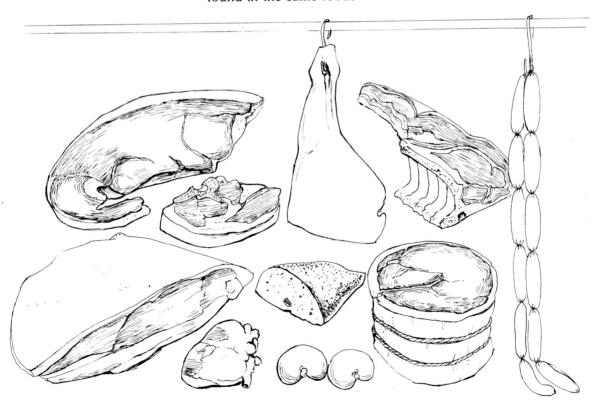

Potassium-rich foods are fruit and fruit juices, meat, milk, natural yoghurt, potatoes and fish. Blood plasma contains high sodium and low potassium levels; red blood cells have a high potassium level with little sodium. These two minerals help to maintain the water balance of the body.

The *magnesium* content of the body is in the bones and teeth for the most part, and the rest is found inside the cells where it is involved in phosphorus metabolism. High protein diets supply sufficient magnesium and increase efficiency of absorption of the mineral. Dolomite and Aminochel Dolomite, mined far beneath the earth, are popular supplements which supply both calcium and magnesium in correct proportions. These are suitable for both vegans and vegetarians.

Iron is necessary for the formation of haemoglobin, the red pigment which carries oxygen through the bloodstream in red blood corpuscles. Lack of iron causes anaemia and women tend to lose iron through heavy menstrual bleeding. Fresh, raw vegetables in at least one meal a day ensure that vital vitamins and minerals are not boiled away. Try to use iron saucepans and steam or lightly fry vegetables at all times.

Zinc sources are liver, kidney, most meats, fish, (especially oysters), and green, leafy vegetables. This element is removed from food in refineries. Zinc is vital to the functions of many organs.

Iodine is found most prevalently in seafood and kelp (seaweed). Iodine in the body is concentrated in the thyroid gland, a small organ at the front and base of the neck. Iodine forms an essential part of the hormone secreted by the thyroid gland.

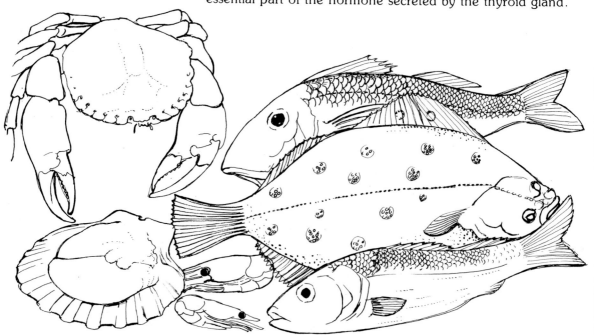

Copper sources are fish, liver, kidney, heart, brain, nuts, seeds, vegetables and prunes. It aids in formation of the red haemoglobin pigment.

Chromium and *manganese* are other essential trace elements which are removed from natural foods in the refining process. Good chromium sources are: dried brewer's yeast, black pepper, cheese, liver, wheat germ, beef; butter, oysters, shrimps, grain and cereal products. The peeling of vegetables can remove a high percentage of the chromium present. Manganese-rich foods are grain, cereal, pulses, leaves (tea), and fruit. Heart disease has been linked with low manganese levels in food and body tissues.

Selenium sources are cereals, nuts, vegetables, fruits, seafoods, liver and kidney. Selenium is destroyed during the refining process and there is some evidence that selenium deficiency is related to cancer and arthritis.

Minerals have to undergo a process called chelation in order to be absorbed into the body to function properly. A true biological chelate consists of a mineral surrounded by amino acids. Natural chelates are chromium and selenium in yeast, iron in haemoglobin, zinc in insulin, magnesium in chlorophyll, calcium in milk, iodine in kelp and cobalt in vitamin B_{12}.

There are those minerals which the body does not require as they induce poisonous effects. They are mercury, cadmium, lead and arsenic.

Lead is introduced into the body through water carried in lead pipes and from car exhausts. If you have lead pipes for drinking water, let the tap run for at least one minute before any is taken for drinking or cooking. Lead will accumulate in the water which has been sitting in the pipes for long periods.

You cannot afford to abuse your body and then expect to cure yourself with synthetic vitamin supplements, which themselves are deadly drugs.

'The eating practices of most people are matters of habit and custom, rather than of intelligent planning. Our people are influenced more in their eating by advertising than they are by a knowledge of foods. They eat what has been made to "taste good", rather than what is truly good. They eat foods which they know contain poisons – chemical preservatives, coal tar dyes, artificial flavourings, etc, with no thought of these poisons, and reject good foods simply because they have not learned to eat them.'

(*Superior Nutrition*, Herbert M Shelton)

Whole foods are the key, the missing link. Otherwise, why in this great technological age are hospitals teeming with sick people wanting to be cured of ailments which could have been avoided? I find it ironic, too, that hospitals and schools still serve white sugar . . . and all the other refined rubbish.

Cancer, diabetes, diseases of the brain, nervous system, heart and arteries, high blood pressure and gall stones are increasing. Yes, the pollutants in the air and water are dangerous, but even more sinister is the way in which people have forgotten the laws of nature. The digestion of food, its assimilation of nutrients to regeneration of cells, tissue, blood, muscle and bone, is a unique biological function. Children are practically suckled on colas and synthetic fruit juices. Then there's tea, coffee, alcohol and tobacco consumption, and compulsive eating.

No matter who says that fat is beautiful, the body is not fat unless something is wrong. Fat people either have glandular or similar disorders or in some way they over-eat; that is, they consume non-nutritive foods and place a great deal of strain on the liver and kidneys. You cannot 'overdose' yourself with nutrients if you receive them in their natural form, through fruits and vegetables. There are many nutritious alternatives to meat.

Rennet is extracted from the stomachs of calves and used in making cheese curds. Cream and cottage cheese are rennet-free, as are many other types which are available. There are also cheeses made from vegetable rennet, for vegetarians. Chived boursin, a French cream cheese, brightens the flavour of black-eyed peas. The protein and calcium content of cheese is not altered by heat so this food is very versatile.

Always bear in mind that to have a balanced diet you must eat all types of foods; combinations count.

Tofu is a traditional Japanese food made from drained and pressed soya bean curd. Like soya beans, it makes a balanced protein food when eaten with whole grains. Tofu is easily digestible, free from cholesterol and low in saturated fats.

Seaweed is available in different varieties: nori is Japan's most popular. Nori are thin, layered squares usually placed round rice and egg. Arame is a mild flavoured seaweed best sautéed or steamed with vegetables or cooked, cooled and added to salads. Kombu is used to flavour stock for casseroles and soups as it is quite thick and flat. Wakame is called spinach of the seaworld and is used mainly in salads.

Fulfil your sugar requirements with sweet grapes, dates, figs, sweet apples, persimmons, raisins, well-ripened bananas, mangoes and paw paws (papayas). The preparation of foods is a factor to be considered because often cooking, mashing, dicing and slicing destroy nutritional value. Eat whole lettuce leaves and if you must cut up fruit and vegetables, cut large chunks.

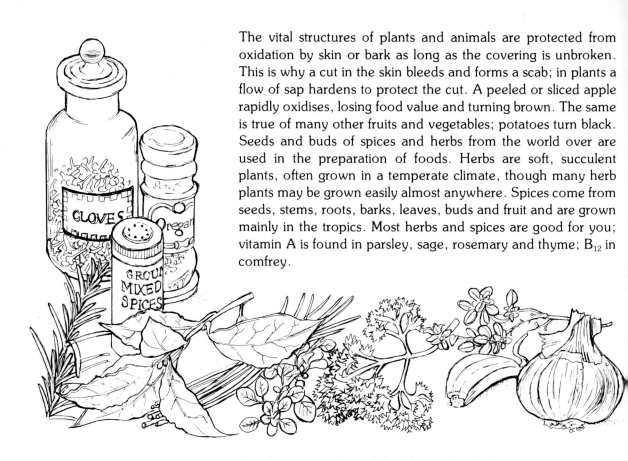

The vital structures of plants and animals are protected from oxidation by skin or bark as long as the covering is unbroken. This is why a cut in the skin bleeds and forms a scab; in plants a flow of sap hardens to protect the cut. A peeled or sliced apple rapidly oxidises, losing food value and turning brown. The same is true of many other fruits and vegetables; potatoes turn black. Seeds and buds of spices and herbs from the world over are used in the preparation of foods. Herbs are soft, succulent plants, often grown in a temperate climate, though many herb plants may be grown easily almost anywhere. Spices come from seeds, stems, roots, barks, leaves, buds and fruit and are grown mainly in the tropics. Most herbs and spices are good for you; vitamin A is found in parsley, sage, rosemary and thyme; B_{12} in comfrey.

Comfrey, a member of the borage family, has been known and used for about 2,000 years. Long ago in rural England it was known as 'boneset' or 'knitback' because of its remarkable powers in mending fractures. It is rich in nitrogen, phosphorus, vitamins A, B and C, and allantoin. Comfrey leaves are gathered, dried and used infused as a tea, for tonic purposes. Fresh, young leaves can be used in salads and can also be applied to the skin to heal bruises, wounds, boils and eczema. Celery, like leeks, is both a vegetable and a herb. File powder consists mainly of sassafrass leaves and is an essential ingredient for gumbo.

If you must drink tea, try to avoid harsh, dyed ones. Too much coffee isn't good for you either; try chicory, root beverage, dandelion, postum or fig drinks.

Tisanes are leaves and flowers used to make soothing, refreshing beverages. Make tisanes from linden, camomile, verbena, anise, orange blossoms, peppermint or fresh mint, sassafrass roots or sarsasparilla. Rose hip tea is rich in vitamin C, as are lemon grass, raspberry leaves, red clover flowers, wild cherry bark, vervain, pennyroyal and nettles. Warmed apple and grape juices also become tisanes when herbs and spices are added.

Apart from your diet, you are affected by whether or not you smoke, the amount of rest you get and the amount of exercise you take. A calorie is a unit to measure energy value, ie the quantity of heat and physical motion that can be obtained from a portion of food. Foods with high calorific values simply provide more heat than similar amounts of low calorie foods. The amount of energy we require varies according to the amount we expend. If too many calories are taken in they are stored in the form of fat (cellulite is just a fancy way of saying fat). Everyone seems obsessed with calories when in fact, if your diet is free of preservatives, depressants and stimulants (alcohol, tea (tannin), coffee (caffeine) and tobacco especially), then you won't have a weight problem anyhow. The same is true if you give up refined and chemically processed foods. Crash diets are not the answer, you gain the lost weight back as soon as you start eating again. Instead of looking to make-up, clothes and money to transform you into a beautiful person, first things first; look after your health.

If your diet is high in carbohydrates and fats and low in protein, you may be more susceptible to hypertension (high blood pressure). Hypertension is sometimes a glandular or hormonal disorder, but mostly is caused by dietary deficiency or imbalance, obesity, hereditary links, stress, birth control pills or water supply.

A word about water

Drink four to eight glasses of water a day to flush out your system, cleanse the kidneys, purify toxic wastes and lessen oily skin blemishes. A glass of warm water with a slice of lemon last thing at night makes you brighter and clearer skinned the next day. This is also useful if you've been out drinking – though the best way to avoid hangovers is not to over-indulge.

Sea water has been used for centuries to cure skin complaints: natural minerals and salts soothe and heal, while wave action stimulates. Pure Evian mineral water speeds the healing of skin when applied in a fine spray mist or with compresses. Water therapies vary from saunas and steam baths, which increase perspiration and deep cleanse, to jacuzzis and whirlpools that stimulate and relax muscles.

Bottled water is usually purer than tap water. Mineral water is water which contains minerals; spring water rises to the surface naturally, under its own steam. Mountain spring water is purest of all. Distilled water is processed so that it contains neither impurities nor minerals. Soft water is very low in natural minerals, while hard water is high in mineral content. Sparkling water has been carbonated with carbon dioxide gas. You can boil tap water, let it cool and keep it in a bottle in the refrigerator, so you always have clean water to drink.

Books to read

if you can get them

Super Natural Cookery, by Jim Corlett

Superior Nutrition, by Herbert M Shelton

Minerals and Your Health, by Len Mervyn

Trace Elements and Nutrition, by Henry A Schroeder

A Professional Dietitian's Natural Fibre Diet, by Margaret Belais Salmon

5 Exercise
is not a specialist field

Thank heavens that women today are discovering their bodies and discarding a lot of hang-ups that have been around for far too long. Somehow physical activity, sweating and sports got given a masculine tag, and women tended to sit on the sidelines to watch and cheer the men on. It is important for every member of society to be as fit and healthy as possible. If the means to be fit are within your grasp, why not do something postive? This method of exercise is not just to shed a few pounds on the thighs, but to make your body work for you, and work efficiently at all times. Every moving part of the body will stiffen if it is not used or moved in the correct manner. Stretching is not only for cats and babies; it increases circulation so that accumulated toxins and lactic acids (which cause muscle stiffness), are carried away. Heat and massage are helpful, although if a muscle is inflamed, apply an icepack.

Be regular

No matter what the choice of exercise programme, all the experts agree that regular exercising increases and improves the capacity of the lungs, strengthens the heart, tones up muscles and accelerates good circulation.

A word of warning

Obviously, if you are out of shape and haven't exercised for ages, you would be wise to start very slowly. Anyone over thirty should consult their doctor before embarking upon a strenuous routine. Even those under thirty who haven't had a recent physical examination should see their doctors first. If you have any medical problems, ie heart disease, high blood pressure, an infectious disease, diabetes or excessive obesity, seek your doctor's opinion before taking the plunge.

In some cases, people have torn ligaments or suffered heart attacks because they tried to do too much, too soon. Body maintenance is painless if you start slowly and work at a pace that suits you best. Firm figures and physical fitness are not the only rewards of an exercise programme. Women in control of their bodies can control their lives to a much greater extent. The mind becomes more alert through the discipline of exercise and

you become more confident and less susceptible to stress and strain.

Swimming and jogging are total exercises in that they develop many muscles, making them supple, yet solid. Swim at least twice a week, if not every day.

Aerobics

Swimming, jogging, cycling and running are typical aerobic exercises. Aerobics, first developed for military training, also include many popular sports. All forms of aerobic exercise demand plenty of oxygen, so they make you work hard; there is a points system by which you gauge your progress. In aerobics you also make a note of your pulse rate and thus your heart-beat, although you can see and feel the differences in yourself.

Don't rush it!

It is always best to warm-up slowly before and wind-down slowly after exercising. Sudden relaxation may cause nausea and dizziness; these symptoms can also be a sign of over-exertion. If you don't think you can run, go for a walk whenever possible or take the stairs briskly, at every opportunity. Strong, flexible shoes are a must for jogging, along with loosely fitting clothing and a good comfortable/supportive bra. Increase distance and speed gradually, walking, then running. Swing your arms and move naturally with a good posture. Avoid pavements as the shock of your feet hitting hard surfaces can result in inflammation of muscle tissue. Jogging is excellent for those who are prone to varicose veins. The contractions and relaxations of the leg muscles squeeze the veins and pump the blood upwards to the heart.

Cycling is good for leg muscles and, if you don't have a bike, lie back on the floor, legs in the air, and pedal as if you are riding.

Yoga

Yoga was devised about two thousand years before the birth of Christ. The word 'yoga' can be translated from Sanskrit as 'union', or the merger of the universal soul with the individual soul. Through bodily and mental self-discipline, one can attain a

union with divine consciousness or Sahmadhi; this is self-realisation. Yoga isn't a religion; it is, however, a spiritual exercise. Hatha Yoga is the most perfect of all home exercise systems because it requires little space and no apparatus. Hatha Yoga teaches meditation, relaxation and the lost art of breathing properly. Shallow breathing utilises about one tenth of the lung capacity, thus people suffer from headaches, fatigue and mental sluggishness.

Tai Chi also stresses flowing, rhythmic body movements and is a healthy system of exercise to develop your co-ordination, balance, flexibility and mental concentration. In advanced stages, Tai Chi can be used for self-defence.

Judo, karate, jujitsu and aikido are excellent forms of exercise which improve balance, strength and endurance.

Go with a group

Group sports are to be recommended, but even some of these need to be supplemented with all-over body exercises.

Lift weights and sagging flesh in a gym. Gymnasiums are wonderful discipline and they offer a wide range of equipment, often plus sauna and jacuzzi facilities.

Dance is a particularly painless form of exercise. Dance combines personal expression with discipline so it has something for everyone. Dance classes offer a variety of choices from jazz, tap, disco, jazz ballet, classical ballet, to belly dancing. Exercises for warming-up are an essential part of the dancer's routine and these can be done at home, in between classes.

Everything must be done regularly and in a disciplined way. Don't race out into the cold after exercising as this causes undue stiffness. A hot bath before you begin will increase flexibility and a hot bath afterwards is ideal for cleansing and relaxing.

Cold water is invigorating; it tightens and tones muscles and stimulates blood circulation. Get into a warm bath and gradually make it cooler; don't jump right into freezing temperatures or you'll shock your system. Don't stay in cold water for more than six minutes; after that you begin to lose body heat.

Don't eat heavily before exercising and never wear anything too tight or binding. Don't give up either, at the first sign of stiffness; the best remedy is moderate exercise. It is wise to get lots of rest and always drink plenty of water.

Come on – relax!

Relaxation is a sort of safety valve, a way of releasing tension, which is caused by stress. There are many ways of relaxing: reading a good book, soaking in the bath, watching a film, listening to music, and so on. Physical exercise is also a very useful form of relaxation.

Breathing exercises release tension by bringing fresh oxygen to fatigued muscles all over the body. Empty lungs of stale air altogether by breathing deeply and properly. Sit or stand upright, inhale to the count of four, breathe out to the count of eight. Take in air through the nose and exhale from the mouth. Blow out your stomach as you breathe in and pull tummy muscles inwards when you breathe out; do this for twenty breaths.

To release tension in the head and neck, stand upright with arms behind your back, breathe in deeply, then slowly rotate your head in a complete circle. Repeat in the opposite direction, concentrating on neck muscles all the time. You can sit cross-legged on the floor for this exercise or sit upright in a straight-backed chair, with your arms at your sides.

129

Many Yoga exercises are for relaxation. The Cobra is a Yoga exercise you can do at home. Lie down on a mat or rug with your stomach against the floor and arms to the sides. Relax, and rest head on floor, hands beneath shoulders, fingertips pointing inward. In very slow motion, tilt head back, push hands against floor and begin to raise your trunk, with your spine curved. Keep thighs on the floor and raise your trunk until arms are barely straight, then hold the position for a count of fifteen. Lower trunk, lie down and relax.

Warm-up first

Stretching relaxes and keeps muscles supple, and joints free of stiffness. Stand erect, feet slightly apart and arms at your sides. Then stand on tiptoe and stretch your arms up to reach for the sky, first one arm, then the other, then both together. Stretch and flex as if climbing an invisible rope, about ten times. Flop down, bending from the waist, and bob gently up and down with your knuckles barely brushing the floor.

A great warm-up for back and leg muscles is to kneel with your hands on the floor and stretch out your left leg behind you, lift and hold for a count of five. Repeat ten times and change to other leg.

Another warm-up for legs and trunk is to stand parallel to a sturdy desk or chair. Lift your right foot to the edge of the desk or chair, raise your left hand above your head, touch right hand to right knee. Bend to the right and reach ten times, then repeat on opposite side.

131

Stretch yourself

To stretch inside leg and tighten waist, sit upright on the floor with legs wide apart. Stretch arms high above your head, pull your waist up and point toes. Then lower hands to floor, lean forward on hands; raise legs, stretch, straighten.

Stretch hips by sitting upright on the floor, legs apart, back completely straight. Take hold of your ankles and bend forward, slowly, from the hips. Bend forward only as far as it feels comfortable, then hold the position for no more than three or five minutes. This also stretches inner thighs.

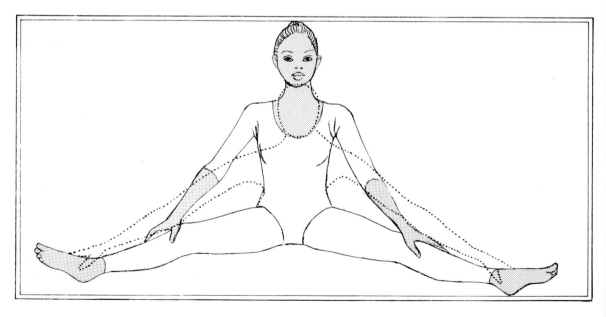

To stretch the waist, stand with hands on hips. Lean to one side as far as you can go, then to the front, other side and back. Do this for about thirty to sixty seconds and don't move your hips as you make the circle.

Put your feet up and wriggle your toes up down, one by one. Hold the other four toes if this proves difficult at first, and wriggle each toe ten times.

Massage is good for you

Massage is good for every part of the body; it relaxes, improves circulation and moves toxic wastes. Always massage legs upwards to assist the blood flow to the heart.

Don't forget your face

There is a great deal of controversy over the benefits of facial exercises; some doctors say that they increase wrinkles, other doctors say that they minimise wrinkles. It is quite true that frowning and scowling can create furrows so it ought to be simple enough to keep the muscles in good tone by not letting them sag into habitual patterns of expression.

Beneath your skin are the bones of your face which cannot be altered unless you have plastic surgery. The facial muscles are ever-changing bundles of fibre; for every muscle that pulls the face into an expression, there is a muscle to pull it in the opposite direction. Muscles work as a team; one will lift an eyebrow, another will lower it. If one half of the team is habitually stretched or flaccid, chances are the other half is continually contracted or shortened; this leads to poor circulation, tightness and shrinkage.

Get those muscles moving to their fullest extent; make a hard O shape with your lips and raise your forehead with eyes wide open. Twist your mouth up, down, side to side, draw down its corners and tighten neck muscles. Smile as hard as you can, and make all kinds of faces; even if you sag somewhere, it's never too late. Adopt a slow and steady pace, though, so that muscles don't get overtired.

And now, lucky you . . . *EXERCISES FOR EVERY BIT OF THE BODY.*

A few facial exercises

To banish a frown: Look into a mirror and, very slowly, pull your brows down, close your eyes into a tight frown. Then open your eyes as wide as you can, lifting your forehead. Repeat six times.

To minimise a double chin or firm a sagging jaw: Press your lips together, smile and push your lower jaw as far forward as possible. Hold the tension and move your jaw from side to side four times, return to starting position and repeat full movement twelve times.

For chin and neck: Tilt your head back slowly, as far as you can, then slowly tilt forward till your chin nearly rests on your chest.

To firm and tighten the neck: Place your hand gently on your throat and tilt your head slightly backwards. Make a hard O shape with your mouth, then pull the muscles around your mouth into a downward smile to make the sound 'ee'. Alternate O and ee shapes for a dozen times.

Tension in the neck and shoulders can lead to irritability and headaches. Don't slouch or hunch over; stand upright, always.

For shoulders: Stand upright, with arms loosely down at your sides. Inhale, lift from your ribcage and raise your shoulders high, and roll them backwards, then down. Repeat in the opposite direction ten times.

On your back ...

Tension, poor posture, poor nutrition and neglect create back problems and abdominal problems, so exercises for the back and spine automatically benefit abdominal muscles. Your spine curves in a natural 'S' shape, so there is no need to over-exaggerate the curve. Don't hold your spine too straight and rigid, either. When you lift things, squat with bent knees, and pick up the weight, straightening the legs, so that you don't strain the back muscles.

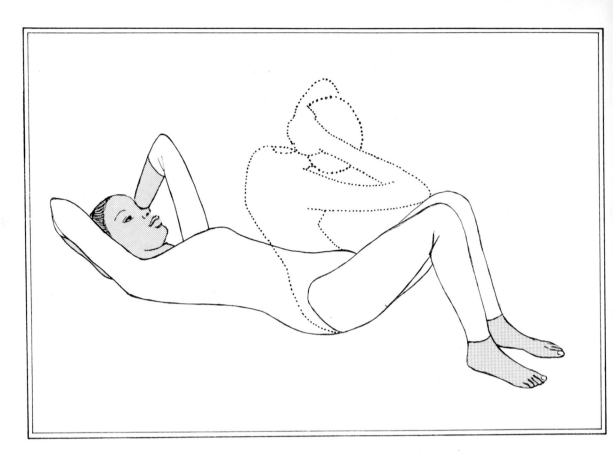

Sit ups: Lie on your back, knees bent, hands behind head. (You can place feet under furniture or have someone hold them down.) Curl up slowly, breathing out. Bring right elbow to left knee, lie back, and repeat on the other side.

Lie on your back (on the floor) with knees bent. Squeeze your buttocks together and flatten your pelvis into the floor. Hold tight for five seconds, then relax. Don't hold your breath with this exercise, breathe freely and let the rest of your body remain relaxed.

Lie on your tummy with a pillow under your abdomen and squeeze your buttocks together, holding tight for a count of five. Release and repeat three to five times.

Dancing and swimming are excellent exercises for the back, particularly the backstroke.

Best breast exercises

Breasts come in all sizes and shapes; they are mainly fat cells, connective tissue, glands and milk ducts. They are not muscles so they depend upon the surrounding pectoral muscles for natural support. Gravity will have its way; a lot depends upon the elasticity of tissue, ageing rate, pre-menstrual tension (which bloats and elongates breasts), pregnancy and childbirth. Excessive weight loss, then gain, or vice versa can affect breasts, as can an ill-fitting bra. If you don't swim, stand upright and practise breast stroke or crawl swimming movements to develop pectoral muscles.

Stand with legs apart, bend forward from your waist and clasp a ruler or rolling pin in your hands behind your back. Pull the rolling pin (or even an empty bottle) up as far as you can, with hands still behind your back. Stretch, lower gently and repeat. Do this ten times or more, as you wish.

Stand with your arms outstretched, weighted with bottles, dumbbells or books. Swing the weights in large circles, but keep your arms straight and the rest of your body still. Circle forwards, then backwards, five times each way.

You can also hold weights straight out in front of you, then open arms and take weights slightly past shoulders; return to starting position and repeat five times.

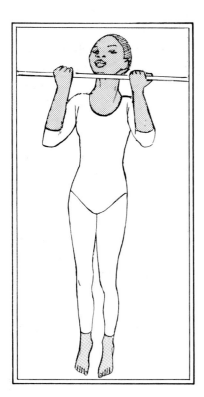

For breasts and arms

Stand or sit on the side of your bed with a pillow in each hand and stretch out arms at shoulder height. Keep your arms straight, swing them together and smash the pillows into each other; repeat ten times and work up to twenty.

Chin-ups strengthen biceps and forearms

Hang from a gymnasium bar for the first few weeks to stretch your body, then try one chin-up and work up to five. Reach for the bar with palms facing you, grasp the bar firmly and pull yourself up until your chin rests on the bar, then let yourself down slowly.

Push-ups strengthen triceps and chest muscles

Lie on your stomach on the floor. Place hands further apart than shoulder width, bend arms with hands turned slightly inward, pressed against the floor. Hold yourself taut and balance on your toes to push with your arms to raise your body off the floor until only toes and palms support your weight. Keep your body straight; inhale when you are flat on the floor, exhale as you push up. Work up to five push-ups, three times a week.

To firm upper arms and lift rib cage

Lie on your back, weights of some kind in your hands, with your hands resting on your knees. Lift the arms alternately up over your head, down to the floor and over to your knees, keeping the arms straight. Do this five times, then with arms together five times.

Improve flexibility and strength in hands by clenching, then relaxing. Hold a rubber ball in each hand and open and close your hands over it as many times as you can.

Well-placed waists

Shape waist and abdomen by sitting on the floor with legs apart, arms back, spine straight; let your arms take your weight, flex your stomach muscles and lift your legs off the floor a few inches for a count of ten.

Bends for waist and back: Stand with feet apart and arms by your side, or one hand on hip. Hold the stomach, push the pelvis forward and bend first to the right, sliding the right arm down the leg. Do the same on the left side and repeat eight times, then try it with arms lifted above your head.

For waist and thighs: Lie face down, bend your legs back and grasp them with your hands at the ankles. Keeping your back arched and head back, rock back and forth, like a rocking chair.

Tighten waist and stretch inside leg by sitting on the floor, legs wide apart and raising the arms high above your head, pulling the waist up. Point toes, and hold for a count of five.

For stomach and leg muscles

Lie on your back, with your legs together. Lift your legs alternately, lowering one as you lift the other as in a walking motion. Begin with five and increase daily.

Lower stomach and inside thighs: Sit on the edge of your bed, feet hanging over from the knees down. Grip a pillow firmly between your feet, place your hands on either side of the bed for balance and, like a see-saw, swing your legs up as high as possible, then down for about two minutes.

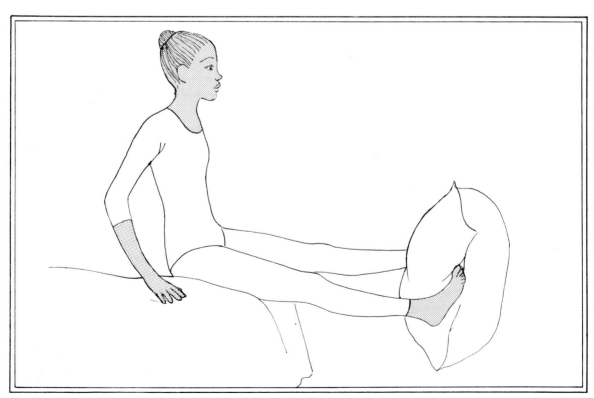

The bottom line

Buttocks and hips: Lie face down on the bed, fold your arms under your chin, bend the knees so that your toes point to the ceiling; keeping the knees bent and slightly apart, lift them and thrust upwards five times, then lower and relax.

Stand erect holding on to the back of a chair. Lift your right leg at the knee and bend your head forward to meet it, then kick that leg back as high as you can with your back arched. Do this five times, then repeat with your left leg.

Kneel with your hands over your head, fingers touching to form an arch. Keep your body facing forward, lower buttocks to touch the floor on the right side, then sit back up and swing over to the left side. Repeat five times each way.

Tips for hips and thighs

Stand straight, hands on hips and bend your right leg, bringing the foot up to your left knee. Straighten your leg slowly to the front; then bring it to the side of your body. Lower, and repeat with the left leg.

Get down on all fours and stretch one leg out to the side, point toes to touch the floor. Keep the arms and body steady and raise leg as high as possible. Keep the leg straight and kick up and down five times, with each leg, making sure that toes touch the floor on the down movement, every time.

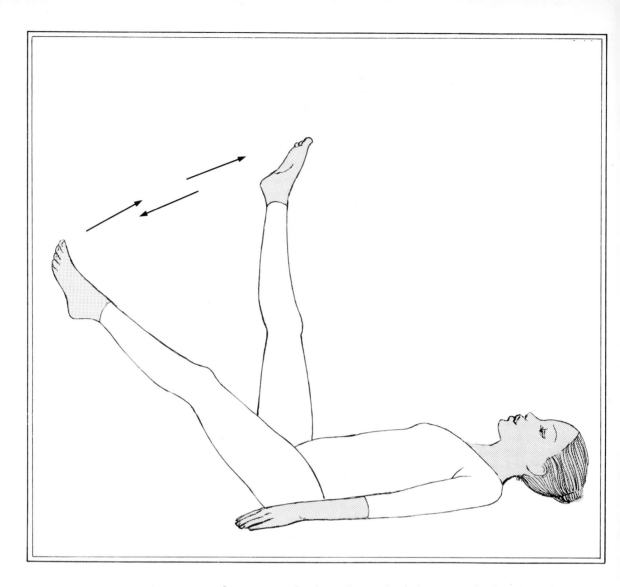

Lie on your back and raise both legs, one higher than the other and scissor-kick. Alternate legs and keep going higher until you've done it about ten times.

Lie on your left side, left leg slightly bent, upper leg straight. Slowly raise your right leg, then slowly lower it and repeat on the other side. Try five the first day, six the second, and so on, up to twenty each side.

For thighs and calves: Stand upright, with feet together, arms straight out in front. Keep your heels flat on the floor and slowly bend at your knees until you feel a pull at the front of your thighs. Clasp your hands behind your neck and hold the position for a count of five; extend your arms again and squat down, heels flat on the floor. Slowly stand straight again.

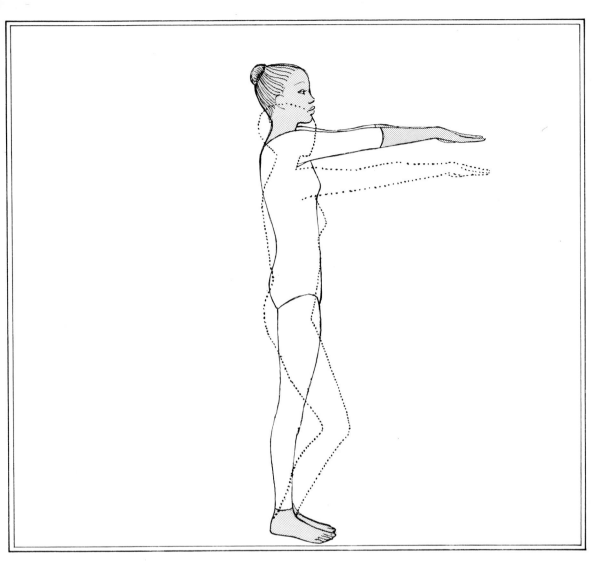

For firmer thighs and calves lie on your back, lean on your hands and lift your hips high off the ground. Move your legs as if riding a bicycle.

Don't forget your feet

Exercise feet by standing on a step or book with toes hanging over the edge. Bend toes down, hold for a count of two, then lift them upwards, hold for two counts and repeat eight times for each foot.

Lie or sit with feet out straight in front. Point your toes and move feet down and outwards in a half-circle. Repeat ten times then do also in the opposite direction, so that feet and toes point inwards.

Kegel exercises

Kegel exercises strengthen the muscle around the vagina and restore good muscle tone to women who have recently had babies. Kegel exercises help to prevent the uterus falling; this occurs if the vaginal muscles are slack. The muscle on the floor of your pelvic area is called the pubococcygeal muscle; it is the muscle that you use to stop the flow of urine. Contract the muscle for a second or two, then release it in a sequence of ten contractions/releases. Do this every day, finally increasing the time of contraction to three seconds or increasing the number of contractions to twenty. Kegel exercises can also be used to intensify orgasm. They can be done whenever you have a few spare minutes anywhere, only you will know.

Now voyager, get into shape and stay that way; enjoy being beautiful.

Books to read

if you can get them

Yoga, by James Hewitt

Our Bodies, Ourselves, Boston Women's Health Book Collective, British Edition by Angela Phillips and Jill Rakusen

The New Aerobics, by Kenneth H Cooper, MD.